AF394528

Please delete address <u>not</u> required before mailing

PHAIDON PRESS INC.

180 Varick Street

New York

NY 10014

PHAIDON PRESS LIMITED

Regent's Wharf

All Saints Street

London N1 9PA

Return address for USA and Canada only

*Return address for UK and countries
outside the USA and Canada only*

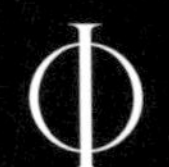

Dear Reader, Books by Phaidon are recognised world-wide for their beauty, scholarship and elegance. We invite you to return this card with your name and e-mail address so that we can keep you informed of our new publications, special offers and events. Alternatively, visit us at **www.phaidon.com** to see our entire list of books, videos and stationery. Register on-line to be included on our regular e-newsletters.

Subjects in which I have a special interest

☐ Art ☐ Contemporary Art ☐ Architecture ☐ Design ☐ Photography

☐ Music ☐ Art Videos ☐ Fashion ☐ Decorative Arts ☐ *Please send me a complimentary catalogue*

Mr/Miss/Ms Initial Surname

Name

No./Street

City

Post code/Zip code Country

E-mail

This is not an order form. To order please contact Customer Services at the appropriate address overleaf.

Larry Fink

by Laurie Dahlberg

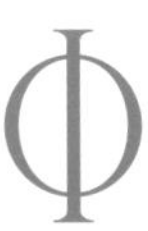

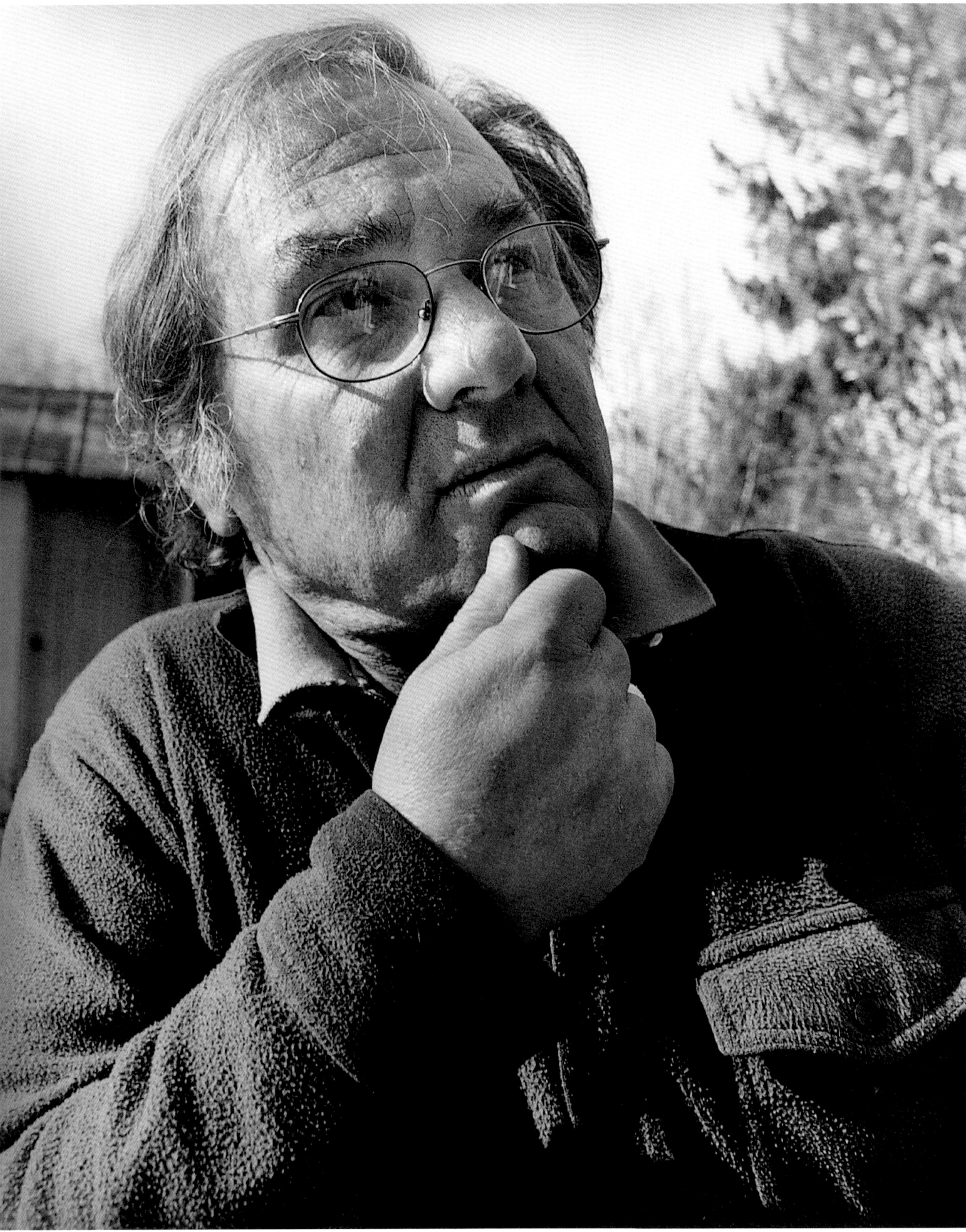

Larry Fink is an intuitively verbal person who can play off aphorisms like a jazz musician plays off flatted fifths. When the standard vocabulary fails, Fink spontaneously coins neologisms, words like 'intrinsicity' and 'instantaneality'. His improvisational statements and phrases are exuberant and sometimes argumentative, but always decisive and sincere. This might serve also as a good description of Fink's pictures. 'Never once have I explored formalism for its own sake,' he says, which he quickly explains as meaning that the emotional content – the human content – always drives the making of his pictures. That Fink also has the astonishing ability of a cardsharp to make the chance ingredients of the space-time moment come out *just so* in the two-dimensional world of the photographic print is necessarily visually compelling. But the formal qualities – the fantastic repetitions of shape and gesture, the slicing vectors of shadow and light that direct the eye to the small, pungent detail – are ultimately conscripted in service of the human element. Moreover, Fink will tell you that the virtuosity of his compositions has little to do with foresight, technical manipulation or practically any method of control on his part. Certainly forty years of experience in photography has made him a master of his tools, so much so that the technical operations are now so natural as to be invisible. But Fink insists that if he really relied fully on his knowledge and experience, the pictures would be failures – they would be too slick. Instead, he honours intuition, improvisation and chance. There is no knowing, he explains, except in knowing that he should 'just relax

and make some pictures'. It's all about instantaneous discovery.
You test your luck and cultivate the givens, much like everything else in life.

A large share of lucky improbabilities marked Fink's path into
photography as an intellectually curious, disaffected teenager
on Long Island. Born in 1941, and raised by his middle-class,
Jewish, leftist parents to relish social vitality, political struggle
and creative expression in many forms, Fink was indifferent to
the promises of the get-ahead, post-war culture of the 1950s.
When it began looking like he would either drop out or be
kicked out of public school, his parents wisely transferred him
to an arts high school. By the time he graduated, it was clear
that the usual sequence of life events plotted for young, white,
middle-class males of the day was not in his future.

Fink and a neighbourhood friend started fooling around with
photography when Fink was about thirteen, building an enlarger
from a cardboard box and making some pictures. His parents
gladly encouraged the expressive sensibilities of their quasi-
delinquent son. His father, an insurance man, had clients who
were artists, including the aging social realists Moses and Raphael
Soyer, who had become family friends. The Finks regarded art
as an honourable profession, particularly when it was in the
service of a social vision. Fink remembers his mother's enthusiastic
reaction to his earliest pictures of 'some daffodils or whatnot'.
From that time on, Sylvia Fink supported her son's photography
with the full force of her considerable energy.

But how were radicalized young men, circa 1958, to transform
their half-formed aspirations into functional creeds and paying
jobs? College, a staging area for this or that career, seemed only
to defer real experience, so Fink dropped out after a few months
and joined a group of 'poets, thieves, goofers – junkies all' living
in subterranean splendour in a basement apartment on Mac-
Dougal Street in Greenwich Village. There he cultivated a kind

of Bohemian pictorialism in his photography, making romantic pictures of the indolent, hand-to-mouth lifestyle of his crowd – young men and women sleeping in cots and on dirty blankets on floors, lounging on broken furniture, smoking, playing guitar. From there, Fink and some cohorts took leave of the city and headed to Mexico to work on a movie being shot by some French acquaintances. The movie never got made, Fink got arrested crossing back into the US and ended up on parole for five years. But he was getting experience.

Fink credits a wise parole officer with diverting him from a squandered life, and a generous priest for getting him his first paid job in photography: hence his respect for grass-roots social involvement and activism. In the early 1960s in New York, working first for the Lexington School for the Deaf, then for an agency that supplied photographs to the Catholic press, Fink operated in a journalistic mode, making earnest pictures about worthy human subjects. Although Fink had begun to develop a good visual and technical command of the tools of black-and-white photography, he felt himself more passionately involved with the message than the medium. He now puts this down to the influence of his mother, who never liked aesthetic self-indulgence. Neither did Fink particularly care to meet other photographers at this time, owing to a youthful insecurity that operated in disguise as youthful pride.

Of course, Fink knew the work of the great photographers of the picture-magazine era, who were then reaching new audiences through the post-war boom in publishing. His dad bought him Henri Cartier-Bresson's *The Decisive Moment* (1952) and *The Europeans* (1955), and he admired the politically engaged work of W. Eugene Smith, the tormented leftist photographer whose personal aims so often conflicted with the corporate aims of his editors. And like any serious photographer coming of age in the early 1960s, Fink could not escape the weighty presence of Robert Frank. He bought his own copy of *The Americans* (US edition, 1959), which he hated and loved because of its 'ungenerous' attitude. Frank's approach to his subject was complicated. Fink ultimately came to recognize its admirable personal honesty, although in his eyes it was virtually without joy, which seemed incomprehensible to him.

Yet while Fink was cultivating an image of himself as an independent, who was inspired more by contact with the subject than by any notion of photographic tradition or style, he could hardly avoid testing the hypotheses formulated by the previous generation. Some of Fink's pictures show him following up the suggestions of his elders about what is worth photographing in the world. For instance, his image of a fiercely self-absorbed man striding down Wall Street in the New York night (no. 24) would look at home among Frank's resonant images of American alienation. The improbably absurd humour of a group of carefree little girls walking beneath the graffiti slogan 'WORK IS FREEDOM', photographed through the bars of an iron fence (no. 07), has the wickedly ironic edge of Cartier-Bresson at his most acerbic. Smith's legacy might be in there too, perhaps in Fink's lush tonal sensibility as a black-and-white photographer, as well as in the homage Fink has so often paid to the working people of the world.

Around 1960, Sylvia Fink received a tip from a commercial photographer who had recently fired her admittedly talented son: if Larry really wanted to develop a uniquely expressive view, he ought to study with Lisette Model, a respected and famously uncompromising figure in the small world of New York art-photography. Model, an Austrian Jew who had fled Europe in 1938, was so committed to her own photographic interests that she barely stayed afloat with freelance assignments. To make ends meet, she taught at the New School for Social Research and, with her husband who was a painter, received a circle of private students and artists in her home. True to character, Fink never took part in these group critiques, which included other photographers who are now well known, such as Leon Levinstein and Diane Arbus. Instead, Model came out to see Fink at his mother's house on Long Island. Although this pedagogical arrangement lasted for little more than a year, the experience was a formative one.

Model's instruction mainly consisted of philosophical conversations with Fink about the pictures he was making: dialogues that flowed into discussions of what it meant to be human. Fink didn't know Model's own work at all, and she never showed it to him. They shared similar political views (she was part of the New York Photo League when McCarthyism forced the League to close in 1951), but neither photographer was interested in the expressly narrative documentation of social realities that is sometimes described as 'concerned photography'. Nor were they so interested in the literal. In fact, whether through the influence of his mentor or by way of natural affinities, Fink's photography has some of the surrealist flavour of European photography of the 1930s, particularly the work of Cartier-Bresson, André Kertész and, perhaps most of all, that great explorer of the poetic, unreal *demi-monde*, Brassaï. Like these photographers, Fink came to appreciate public life as an uncanny theatre of chance. Acutely attentive to the visual disjunctures and surprises hidden in the folds of the living moment, he understands the camera's transformation of animate life into picture: shadows take the shape of birds, human gestures synchronize inscrutably with architecture, unacknowledged desires reveal themselves through arrested glances. Absurdity, pathos, grace and wit operate by turns, sometimes passing in an unbroken circuit through a single image.

Yet for all his appreciation of the metaphysics of intuition, the purely physical holds pride of place in Fink's view of human experience. With his respect for the primitive authority of the body, it is hardly surprising that Fink's pictures celebrate our drives to fulfil sensual demands: to compete for food, drink, sex and bodily pleasures of all kinds. Sometimes they show us offering our bodies as objects to be visually consumed, engaging in spectacles of physicality like catwalk modelling, boxing or performing sex for movie cameras. Other times they locate our secret moments of corporeal alienation. A crowd in Fink's pictures is less a group of people than a writhing press of bodies, stretching, gesturing, completing and compounding each other, like refugees from Mannerist painting.

With his heightened sense of the drama of human flesh, Fink has something in common with both Model and her student Arbus, who was even more captivated than Model by the corporeality of others. However, Fink's theatre is not as driven by individual characters, but rather by the actions that animate them and connect them to each other. Under Model's tutelage, Fink learned to trust and appreciate photography as an active principle, as a means by which to negotiate the terms of living in a human body that naturally interacts with other bodies. It's not a matter of the photographer effacing himself so that the object can emerge from the picture in some pure 'essential' form, but of him reacting to his fellow beings with an honest range of feelings: joy, disgust, contempt, wonder, curiosity and attraction. This is a modality Fink now refers to as 'sensual empathy' and, if we want to apply the terms of art, it's what tips the balance of his work away from realism in the direction of expressionism. Unlike many photographers of the social realm, such as the circumspect Cartier-Bresson and Frank, who take up positions as virtually invisible observers when working, Fink is an interactive participant who categorically enters the scene as a photographer with cameras and flash in hand. In this sense, Fink takes after another beloved predecessor and fellow New Yorker, the freelance tabloid photographer (and Lisette Model's pseudo-rival) Weegee.

By the mid-1960s, Fink's freelance career was well under way. Photographing 'incessantly, obsessively' brought him to a point of clarity about what he was doing. Seeking to serve social change and effect political awakening through the visual means in his power – this was an honourable mission. Glad to throw in his lot as a photographer of the revolution, Fink photographed the demonstrations, began teaching photography to inner-city children in community programmes, and curated photography shows at Columbia University for the peace movement. These activities caught the interest of Magnum, the gold standard of picture agencies. Perhaps it was Magnum's formidable, exclusive status as a collective run by the world's most famous photojournalists, but Fink was not ready to acquiesce to success. He preferred to carry on as before, following an intermittent trail of opportunities suited to his notion of acting for the social good. For the moment, making a contribution was better than making a living.

In 1969, external pressure and his own striving ego ultimately led Fink to take his first ambivalent step into the art world proper, when he accepted a show at an emerging gallery in SoHo. Over the next few years he received increasingly prominent shows in the US and abroad, including a one-man exhibition in 1979 at the Museum of Modern Art in New York. An exhibition at MoMA seemed somewhat paradoxical, as Fink still speaks with some warmth about the rumour that in the 1960s the Museum hired CIA-trained curators and conspired with the government to keep the work of politically engaged artists off the walls. While Fink welcomed the recognition, he was troubled by his participation in a system so deeply enmeshed in the structures of money and power. Stranger still was the fact that the work attracting this notice consisted of subversive pictures that skewered Manhattan's cultural élite and exposed the dubious veneer of morality that protects the very rich. These pictures would form the basis of Fink's first book, *Social Graces* (1984), a dialectical portrait of high and low culture in the US.

The project proposed itself years earlier when the contrarian Fink, determined to provoke social critique, sought a way to expose the corrupt nature of power that is so well concealed by the benevolent, magisterial stance of cultural leaders. He bought a tuxedo and played the part of a society photographer, insinuating himself into the Olympian world of New York's Museum Mile charity balls, debutante cotillions and art-gallery openings. Having previously used available light in the interest of a non-invasive working style, he now faced the technical problem of photographing low-light parties full of people dressed in black. In 1968, when he was hired to cover a centennial ball at the Metropolitan Museum of Art, he brought along a hand-held flash for the first time. It was, he recalls, an exhilarating revelation of power. By 1972, the black-tie project was absorbing Fink's full energy and focus. Now he began using the hand-held flash almost exclusively, just as he retired the 35 mm camera in favour of the square format twin-reflex.

Having settled on his technical tools, Fink infiltrated these events like the undercover radical he was, filled with a delicious sense of 'wrathful sedition'. In the tradition of artists like Francisco de Goya, George Grosz and Otto Dix (all personal heroes), he ran this gauntlet of parties in order to bear witness to the baser instincts of our social betters. Lust, vanity, mendacity, avarice, gluttony – his subjects displayed them all, just like the bloated patricians of ancient Rome. But if Fink really stands by his philosophy of 'sensual empathy', we're correct in sensing a complicating factor in these pictures of captains of industry, their leathery wives and concupiscent offspring, in that the photographer could recognize many of his own frailties and appetites in theirs. Fink's immersion in the unfolding scene thus suggests not so much a clinically detached observer as an experienced participant – one who is therefore qualified to testify. A few of the black-tie pictures exhibit an unexpected tenderness, pictures taken at a demure distance that return a respectful acknowledgement of the loneliness and psychic pain that afflicts human nature, even for those of vast privilege. Fink was not the only photographer working at these kinds of parties at the time (occasionally he would run into Lee Friedlander or Garry Winogrand, who also recognized alcohol-fuelled gatherings of the 'beautiful people' as events loaded with ambiguity and interesting visual potential), but he was undoubtedly the most direct about his adversarial reasons for doing so.

After several years, a change in Fink's living situation presented him with the means to draw this portrait of American wealth even more sharply. In 1974, well into the black-tie project, Fink and his wife, the painter Joan Snyder, bought an ancient, dilapidated farm in the backwoods of eastern Pennsylvania. The postal address was Martins Creek, a remote village that serves the area with a church, gas station, corner store and post office. What he found there was a community of hard-working farmers who owned nothing but their vehicles and a parcel of land (if that), and who lost a bit of their capital and their health every year. These descendants of Jacksonian democracy bore witness to the fact that the egalitarian dreams of the founding fathers were hopelessly at odds with the methods and needs of an aggressively capitalist society. In other words, Fink found a community that answered his romantic yearnings for authenticity and confirmed his bleakest political beliefs about contemporary America. Still, Fink was cautious about thinking of his neighbours as a possible photographic subject. While he knew the two groups of pictures would draw each other into a natural dialectic, this was not the reason he began to take photographs of the people at Martins Creek.

Over several years he came to know his neighbours as friends, particularly the Sabatine family, who invited Fink and his young daughter Molly to their casual gatherings and ritual celebrations: birthdays, graduations, Fourth of July cookouts, anniversaries and so on. By the time he was ready to photograph them, and they were willing to be photographed, he had developed an organic understanding of their collective life and, above all, valued his relationships with them as individuals. Fink

acknowledges the photographer is in an impossible situation
when representing his fellow human beings: he cannot help
but have a personal will and intention that can never be fully
transparent to the person he is photographing. More to the
point, the picture will go on to have a life of its own that
neither the photographer or the subject can predict or control.
Fink accepts this as the burden he must bear in exchange for
the chance to be the translator of something meaningful and
personally 'real', but ultimately elusive and ephemeral. So the
process of photography requires an act of faith on the part of all
involved: photographer, subject and viewer. Fink's subjects are
usually knowing and complicit, like his neighbours in Martins
Creek. But even when this is not the case, as in many of the
black-tie photographs, Fink insists his search is an honest one.
'There's something in me that is so oddly natural about photographing,' he says. 'As soon as I put a camera in front of my
eye, there's something in me that remains innocent ... even if
I'm fully aware of its result, my search is innocent.'

As in the black-tie pictures, Fink was attracted to the spectacle
of sensual indulgence at Martins Creek, but here it is at the
level of kitchen-table buffets with their huge sheet cakes, cans
of soda, punch bowls and heaps of popcorn, or Legion Hall bars
loaded down with bar glasses, pitchers of draught beer and
overflowing ashtrays. Unlike the resolutely adult culture of the
black-tie parties, the rural social circle includes babies, pension-
ers and everyone in between, but this does not necessarily reduce
the Martins Creek parties to a sweet and wholesome version of
the black-tie events. In fact, part of the appeal of the *Social
Graces* project lies in Fink's consistent portrayal of sensuality as
a double-edged faculty. Like their black-tie counterparts, the
Martins Creek people cultivate the human appetite to both the
delight and the detriment of the body, but they are less likely
to cheat time with the luxury of cosmetic surgery or health-
club workouts than they are to receive sub-standard health care.
The ambivalent future of the healthy young bodies of Martins

Creek children is manifest when compared with the forms of their physically haggard elders. Life can be short and brutish; pleasures need to be taken where they're found, usually in the shelter of the family.

Following the critical acclaim for *Social Graces* (1984), Fink found himself struggling against his own success and newly golden reputation, resenting the expectations it heaped upon him, but nevertheless fearing to lose that status. At about the same time, his marriage to Snyder was coming to an end, all of which contributed to his decision to spend some time in Europe. This liberating break from US culture brought him back to the 'core need' that made him take photographs in the first place: his compelling questions about our experience as wonderful, flawed human creatures. When he returned, he immersed himself in freelance work (which he has never abandoned), investing assignments with the same importance and values that guide his personal work. With his abiding sense of proletarian worth, Fink takes pride in being a working photographer, as opposed to a rarefied artist who 'soars only in his own stratosphere'. 'A lot can be said for exploring your own potential,' he observes, 'but there is also some contradiction to the notion of that exclusively being freedom.' Fink looks for answers to his questions about human sensuality and desire in many places: at a convention of the religious right, in corporate conference rooms, or backstage at a Versace couture show. Some of Fink's greatest pictures come from taking photographs at weddings and bar mitzvahs, and from assignments for any number of magazines.

In some cases, small magazine assignments have led to Fink's richest subjects, like the boxing series he began on assignment for *Manhattan, Inc.* That first experience of taking photographs at a small gym in Catskill, New York, in 1987 recalled some long forgotten, purely visceral and wondrous excitement that Fink had felt as a child listening to boxing matches on the radio, but which had been lost for him in the transition of the sport to television. He spent the next ten years taking photographs in the small boxing gyms and rings around Philadelphia, culminating in a book published in 1997. Similarly, Fink's trenchant photography of the fashion world – generously commissioned over the past decade by the very culture he critiques – has been collected in *Runway* (2000). A book tends to crystallize a subject for him, leaving little need to go further once he sees the pictures in their distilled, edited form. Nevertheless, Fink admits he still does parties: 'While I can say I would never photograph another party again, once I get to a party and start my camera moving, with all the people drinking and goggling and goofing and doing stupid or wonderful things, I get interested in photographing again.'

Fink still lives in Martins Creek and he still keeps up with the neighbours. His daughter is now grown up and he has remarried. He maintains the same intense pace of freelancing. In addition to his packed schedule of professional work, he has been teaching photography since 1965 at institutions such as Yale University, the Cooper Union School of Art and, most recently, Bard College. He finds in his students an analogue for his own passions and curiosity about the world, which adds further continuity to his life.

Over the years, Fink has found flesh, and the spirit that animates it, at the heart of most of his work, whether in pictures of waiters, pugilists, underwear models, high-school students, Portuguese fishermen, wedding guests, stockbrokers or elderly women. His profession still absolutely thrills him, and it is his own ebullient, scathing, curious or chastened response to each situation that gives these pictures life. But to forget the viewer would be to betray Fink's principles, for his first theorem is equal access: he will never neglect to put the viewer on the guest list. 'I'm not interested in an oblique art,' he explains, 'though I am interested in oblique terms that may better express very literal ones.' Although he has tempered his expectations for profound, positive political change in his lifetime, he still feels photography is the best way he can serve his old humanistic ideals. Nothing is more basic than the human desire for knowledge and experience, whether carnal, spiritual or something else, and in pursuing the way we negotiate those drives with our fellow beings, Fink will continue looking for larger relevance in the small gestures of individual lives.

 1958 Moses Soyer Studio, New York City.

Fink's introduction to the world of art and artists first came through the painters Moses and Raphael Soyer, who were old friends of his parents. Frequenting Moses' studio in the late 1950s, Fink made this romantic portrait which turns fancifully on the old question of life imitating art. While the uncanny repetition of the model and her denatured elegance have a surreal flavour (one thinks of the hypnotic women of painter Paul Delvaux, for example), this is one of Fink's most lyrical images, made before he began cultivating photography's more disjunctively surreal aspects.

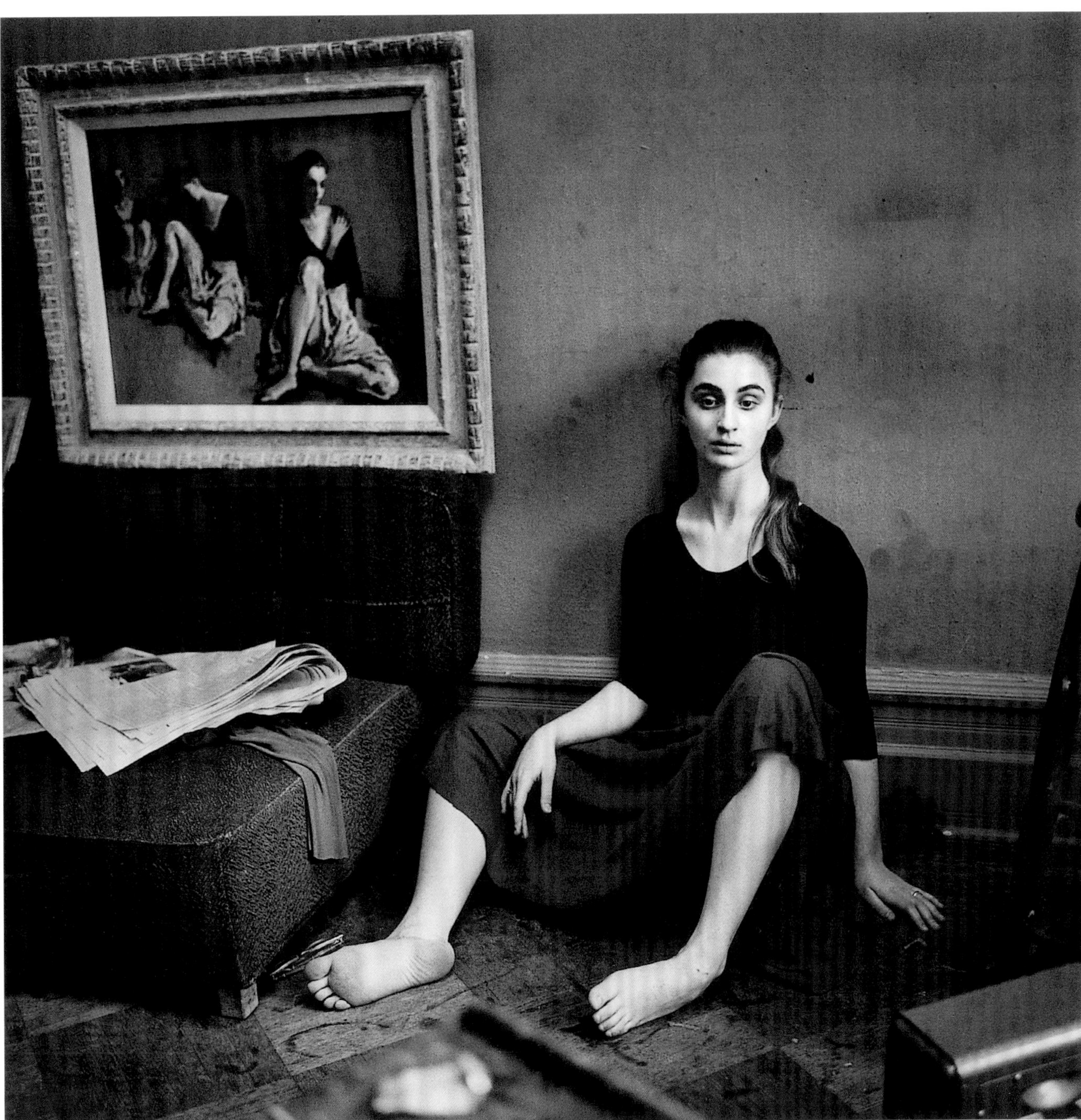

1959 | Jazz, New York City.

As a dedicated disciple of jazz and a serious pianist, Fink spent many hours in the New York jazz clubs of the 1950s and 1960s. This compact picture of an unknown pianist expresses the intensity of a musical performance with minimal visual cues: the black pianist's profile with its line of perspiration and the decisive touch of his hand upon the finely articulated backbone of the keyboard.

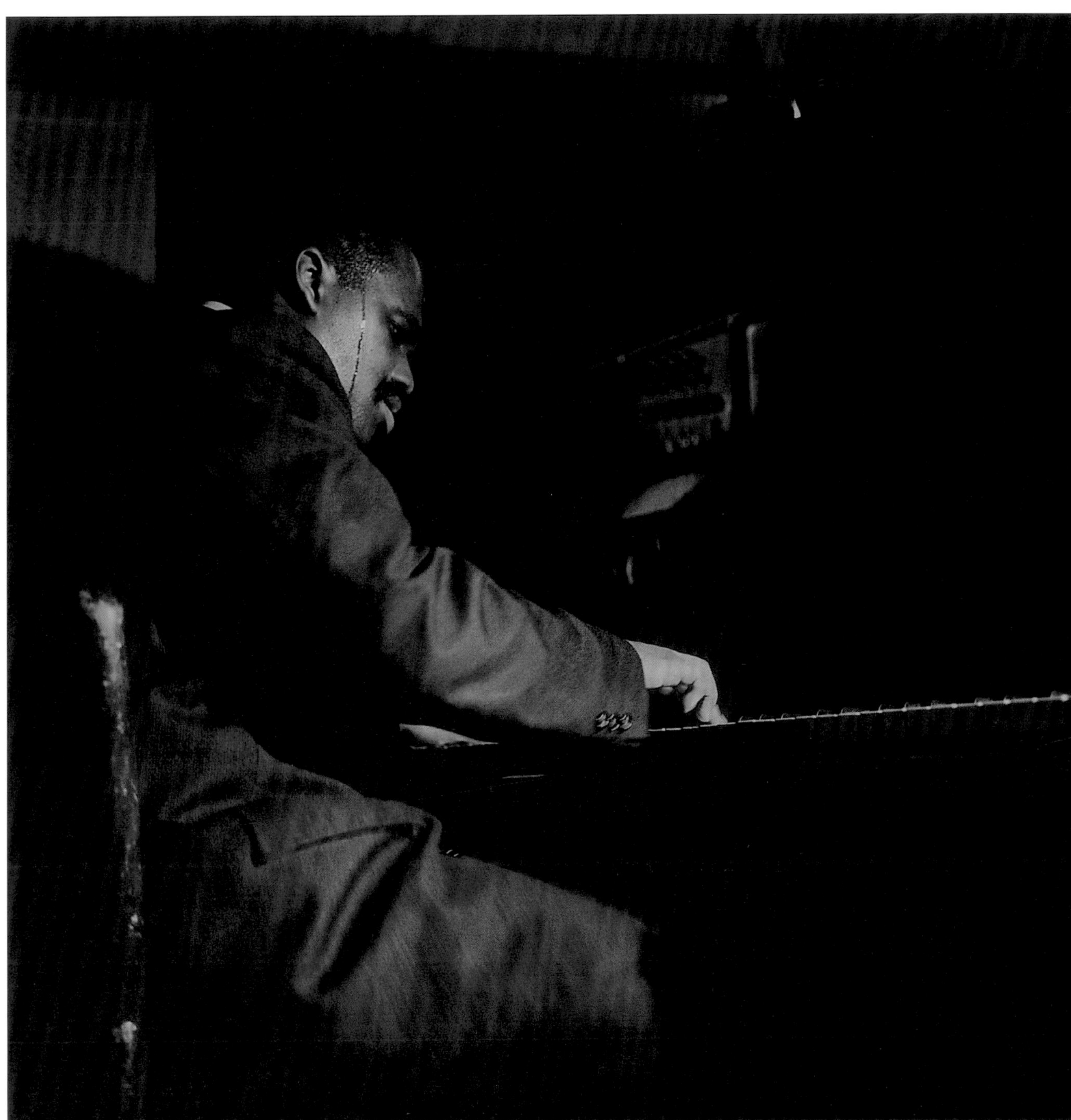

1959

Beatniks, St Louis, Missouri.

Photographing the stylized gestures of two young men in a park, Fink is already anticipating his later interest in the way bodies in three dimensions relate graphically in the flattened space of the photograph. In the years to come, Fink would continue to deepen his feeling for the expressive content (here, the serio-comic, self-assured posturing of young hipsters) while also strengthening the visual impact of the full photographic frame, in particular by learning how to avoid dead space and activating the corners of the picture.

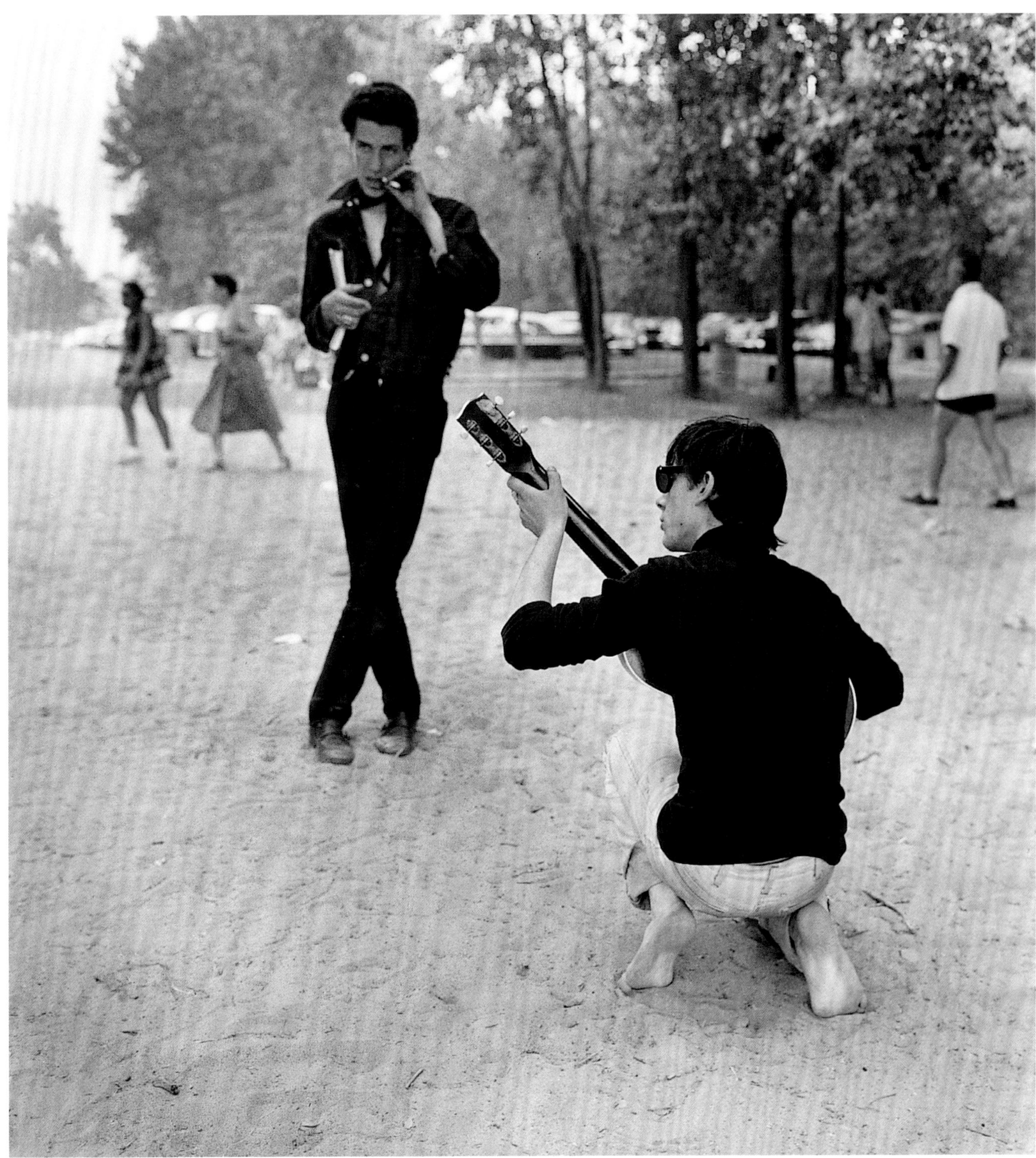

04

1959   Beatniks, Angel of Death, Missouri.

Like many young photographers, Fink began learning his art by document-
ing his own social milieu. This genre of photography came to be called
'personal journalism' by writers describing similar work by photographers
such as Danny Lyon and Larry Clark. In the half-light of a drab room that
looks out upon a sunny landscape, the picture renders both the tense, sup-
pressed energy of youth and the dissipation that often neutralizes it. As a
photographer seeking a more external connection with the world, Fink
would soon set aside diaristic subject matter in his public work, although
he continues to keep a private record of his family.

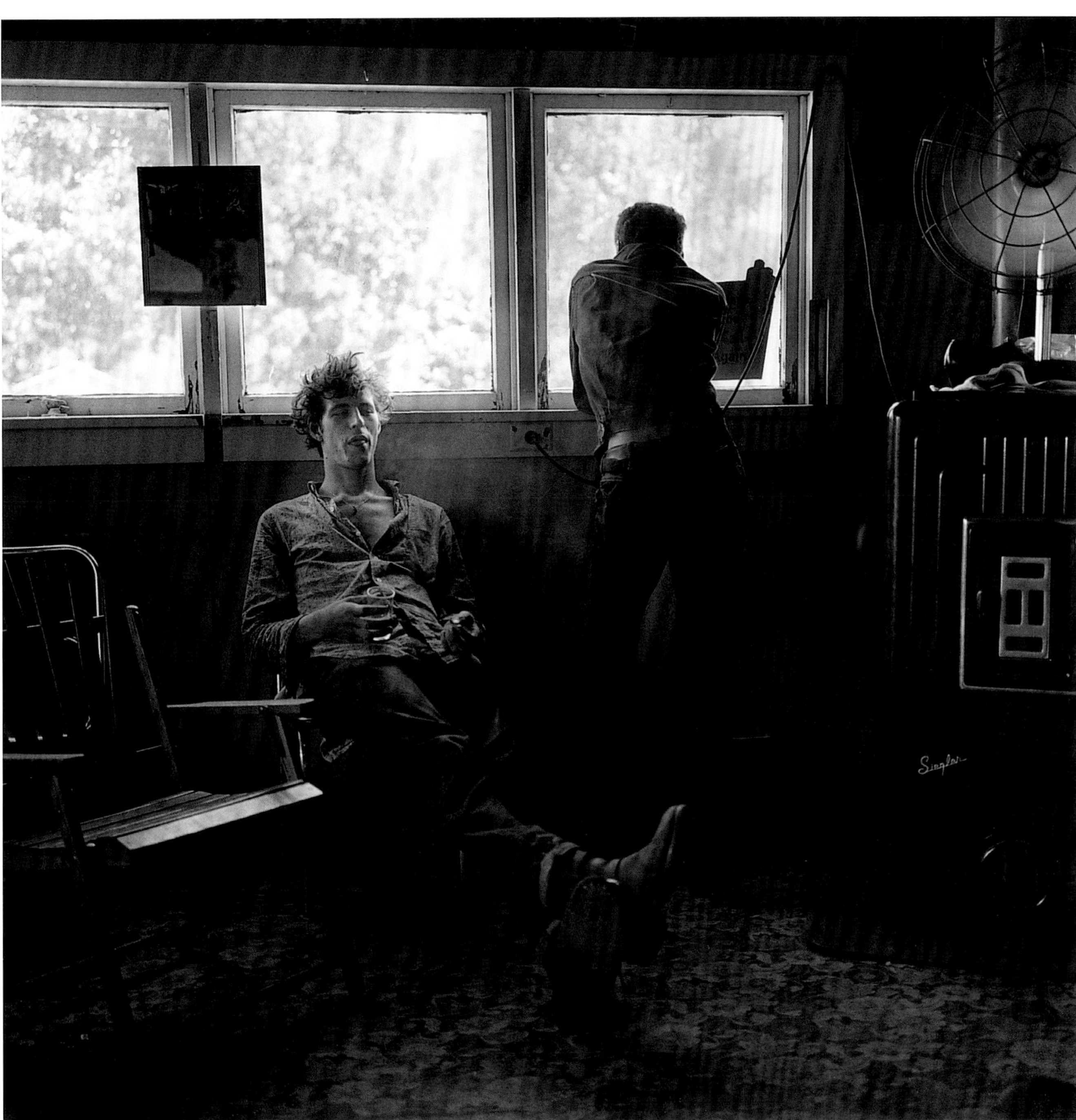

05

1967   The Vatican, Rome.

Fink found this mother and daughter in a chapel at the Vatican: the line for
salvation forms to the rear. With its humour and surrealism incongruously
realized in a setting of sober piety, this image certainly brings to mind the
adventuring wit of Henri Cartier-Bresson, a towering figure whose inspira-
tion Fink unequivocally acknowledges.

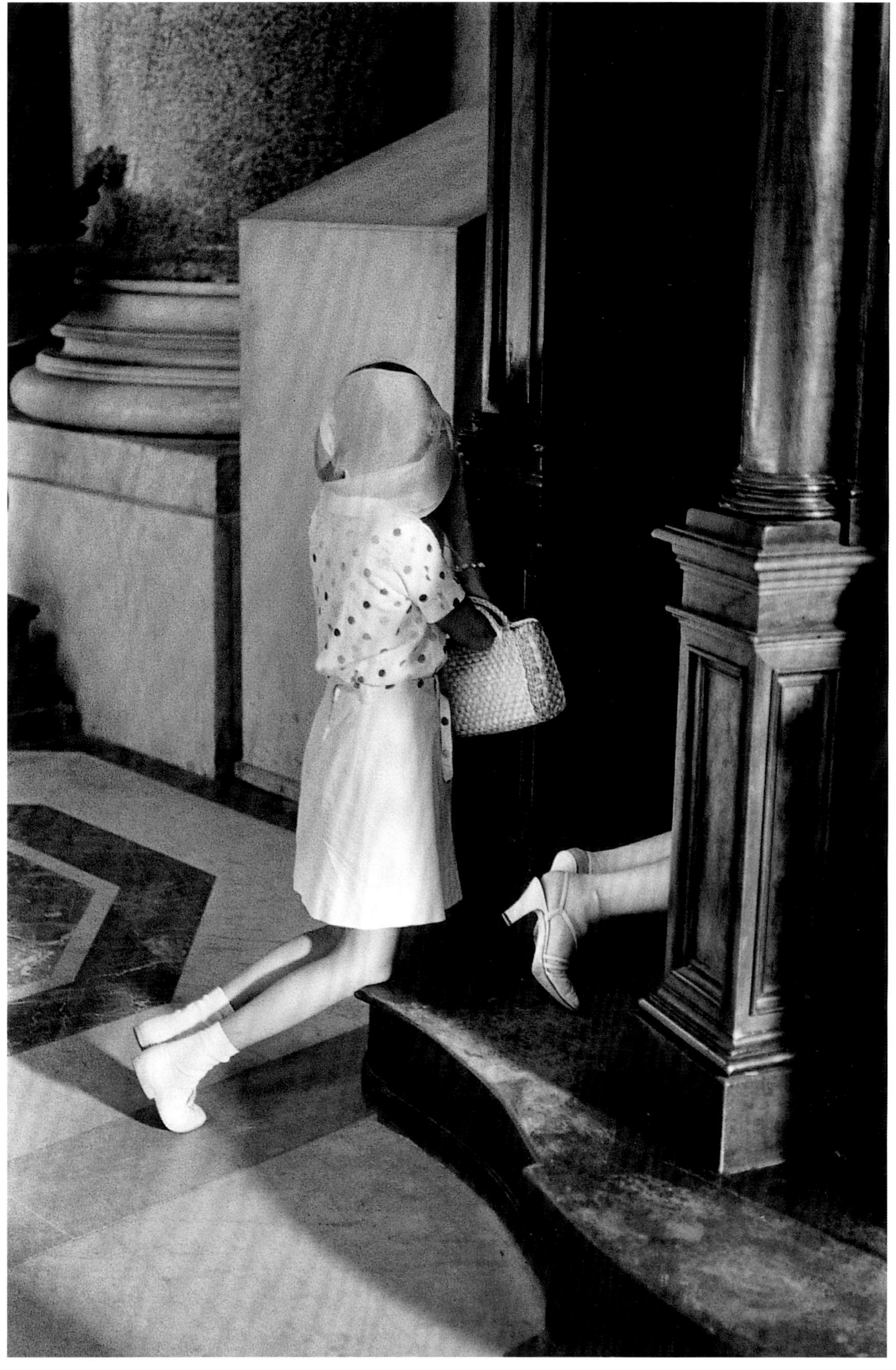

 1967 New York City.

This early picture, made when Fink was still regularly using the 35 mm format, recalls his teacher Lisette Model's interest in the expressivity of those most pedestrian of body parts: legs and feet. Fink manages to draw a telling portrait of a woman without showing her face. Centring her in the vertical photographic frame to maximize the presence and stability of her physical frame, Fink studies her sturdy legs, back and formidable body language – feet spread, hand on hip – and constructs the image of a strident, no-nonsense woman, a real New Yorker.

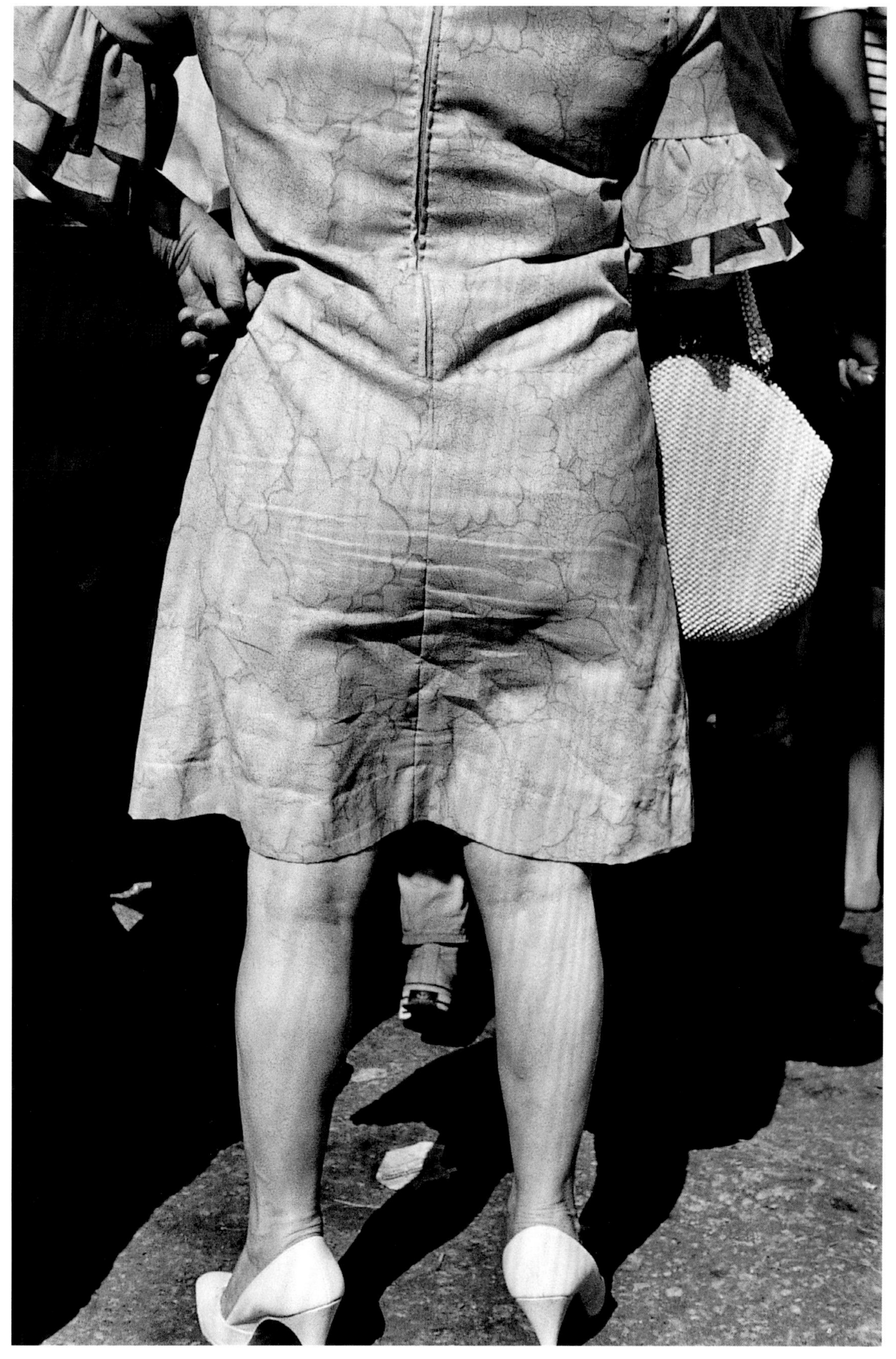

Living in London in 1968, Fink evidently happened upon some competition between the local gods of chance: three girls marching in a blissful cadence beneath the sadly misspelled (and corrected) graffiti slogan 'WORK IS FREDOM'. The abundant signifiers of imprisonment – barbed wire, brick walls, an iron fence and the idea of work, even if it is theorized as 'freedom' – are pitted against the painful sweetness of the three carefree poppets, skipping along the pavement, eating their ice-cream cones. The self-correcting conscience of the graffiti artist mediates the conflict between revolution and conformity. As Fink says of this picture, 'Literature is flawed, but action isn't.'

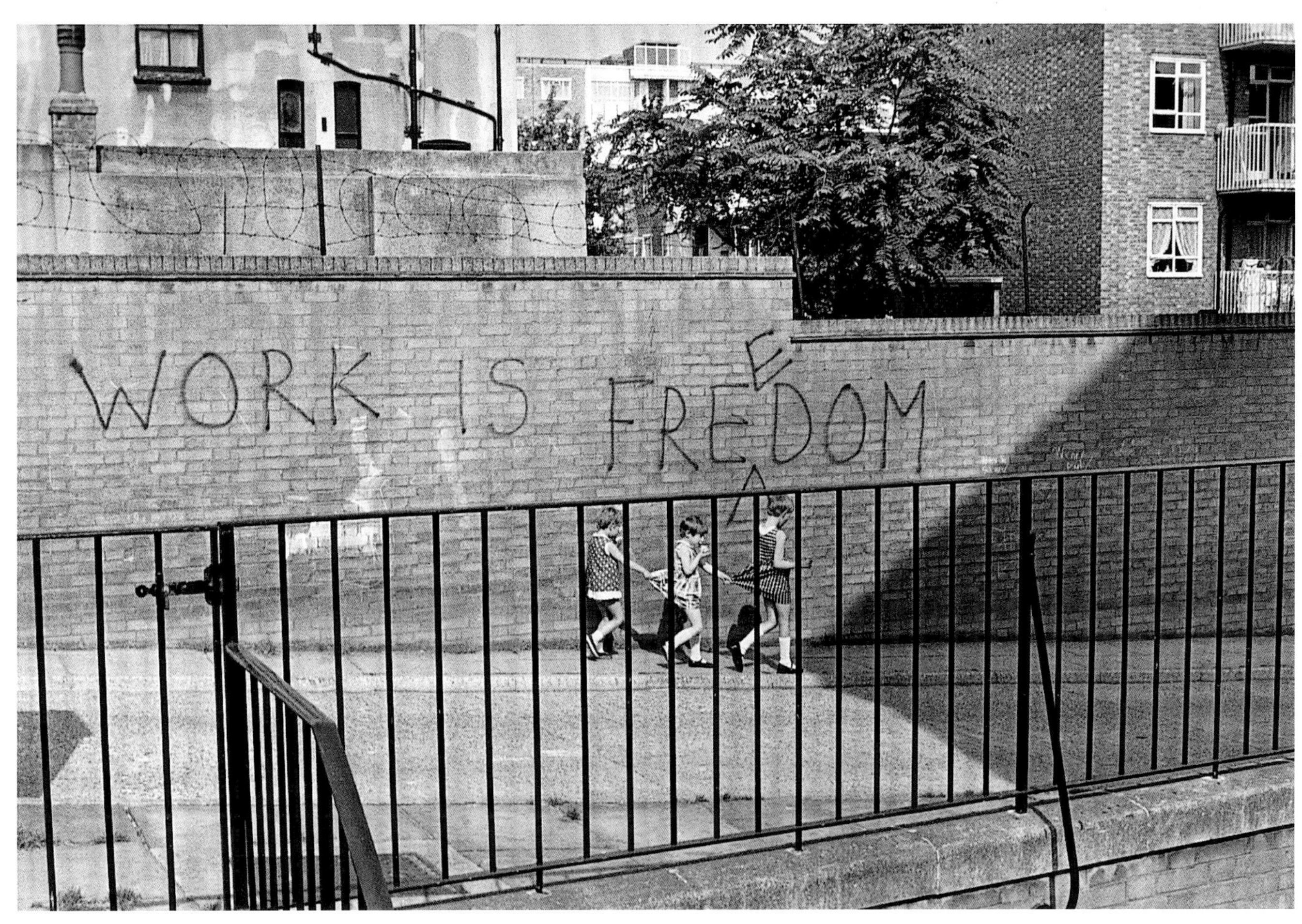

WORK IS FREEDOM

08

15 November 1969   Washington Moratorium, Washington DC.

This picture of the roiling crowd at the 1969 Moratorium march on
Washington, DC is crowned by the luckiest of accidents. Looking
through the darkened optics of the 20 mm lens, focusing on the leader
of the protest raising his fist, Fink was aware of the Washington
Monument rising up behind them, but he could not possibly have
seen the small black helicopter flying menacingly overhead.

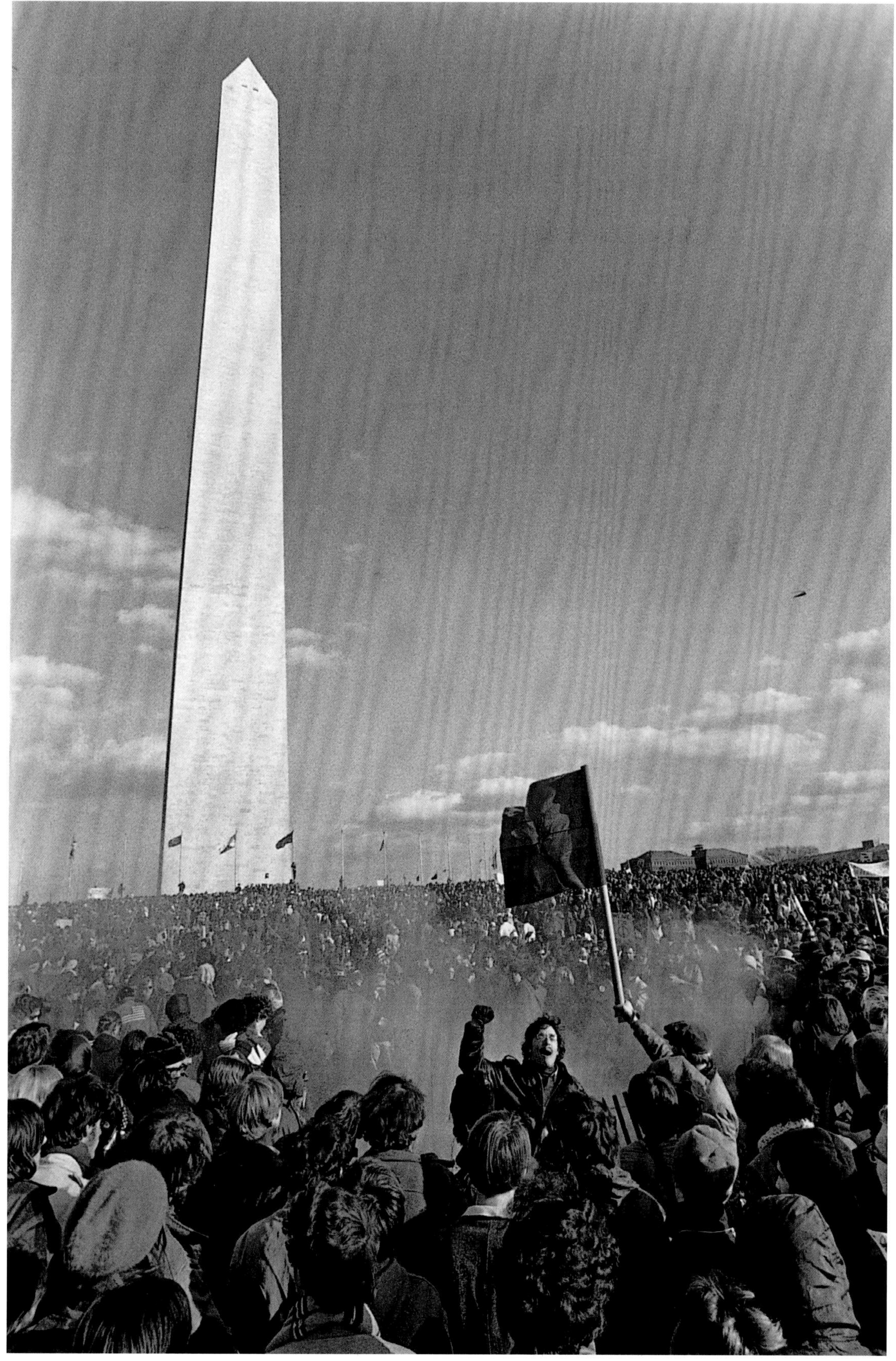

09

February 1975   Washington, DC.

Fink's affinities with European surrealism come to the fore in this picture:
it calls to mind common strategies and conditions of surrealism, such as
the 'making strange' of familiar things and the unease provoked by
depriving body parts of the unifying context of the whole body. At the
centre of a field of matt blacks and dark greys, the flesh of this wrinkled,
mottled fist glows cold and white under the flash, which renders it like
the skin of butchered poultry.

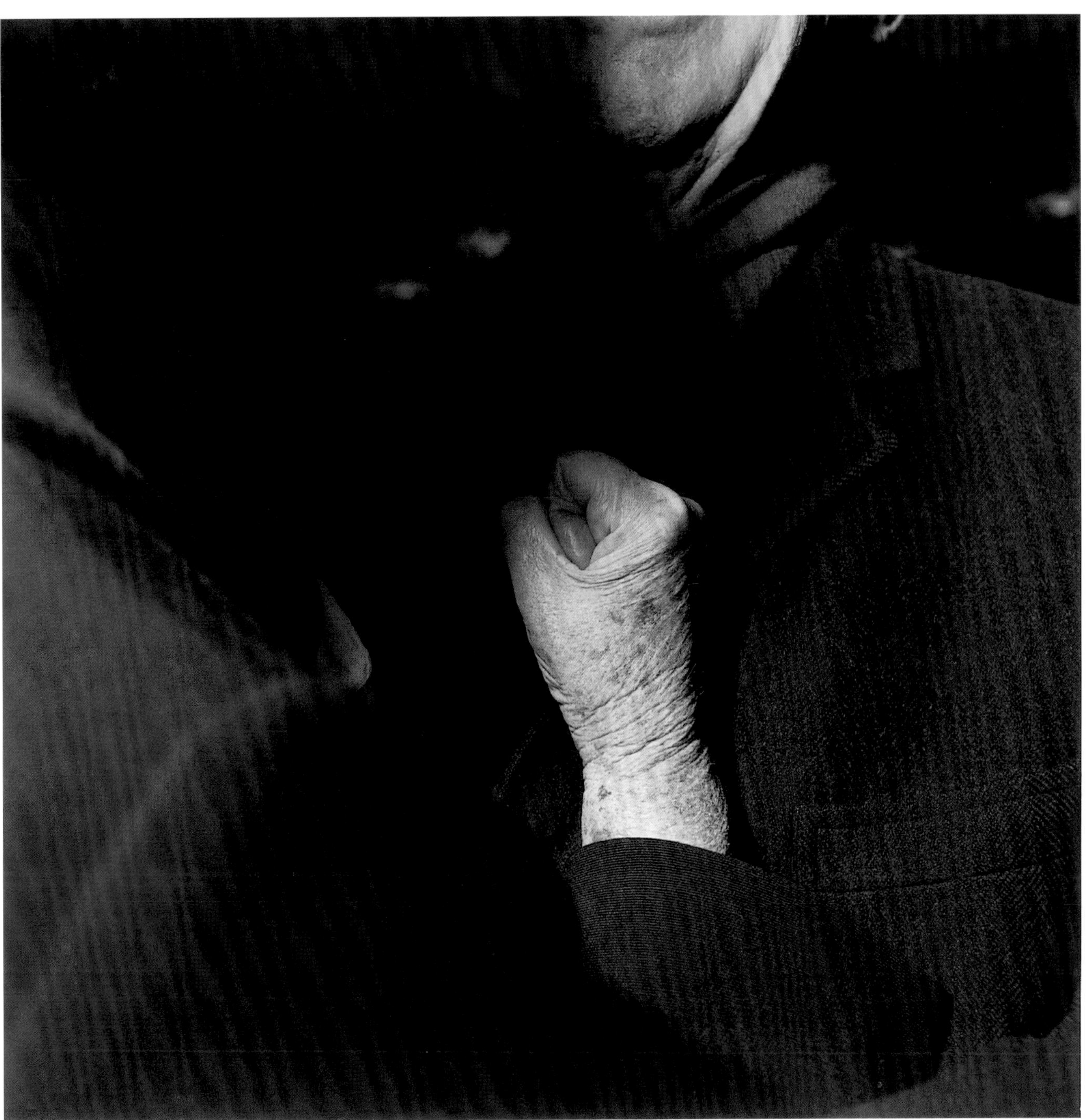

10

April 1977   Pat Sabatine's Eighth Birthday Party, Martins Creek.

The balletic, or perhaps operatic, expressiveness of this picture, used for the cover of *Social Graces* (1984), naturally calls to mind Henri Cartier-Bresson's phrase 'the decisive moment': the instant at which the formal qualities of a picture come together with its expressive content to create an apex of meaning. While Fink's images certainly honour this idea, his work is fundamentally different from Cartier-Bresson's, not least because his flash draws radical attention to both the graphic edges of objects in its path and the photographer's presence. Moreover, unlike Cartier-Bresson's 35 mm field, which is usually classically ordered on a horizontal axis, Fink composes as much for the corners of his muscular square frame as for whatever action is happening at its centre.

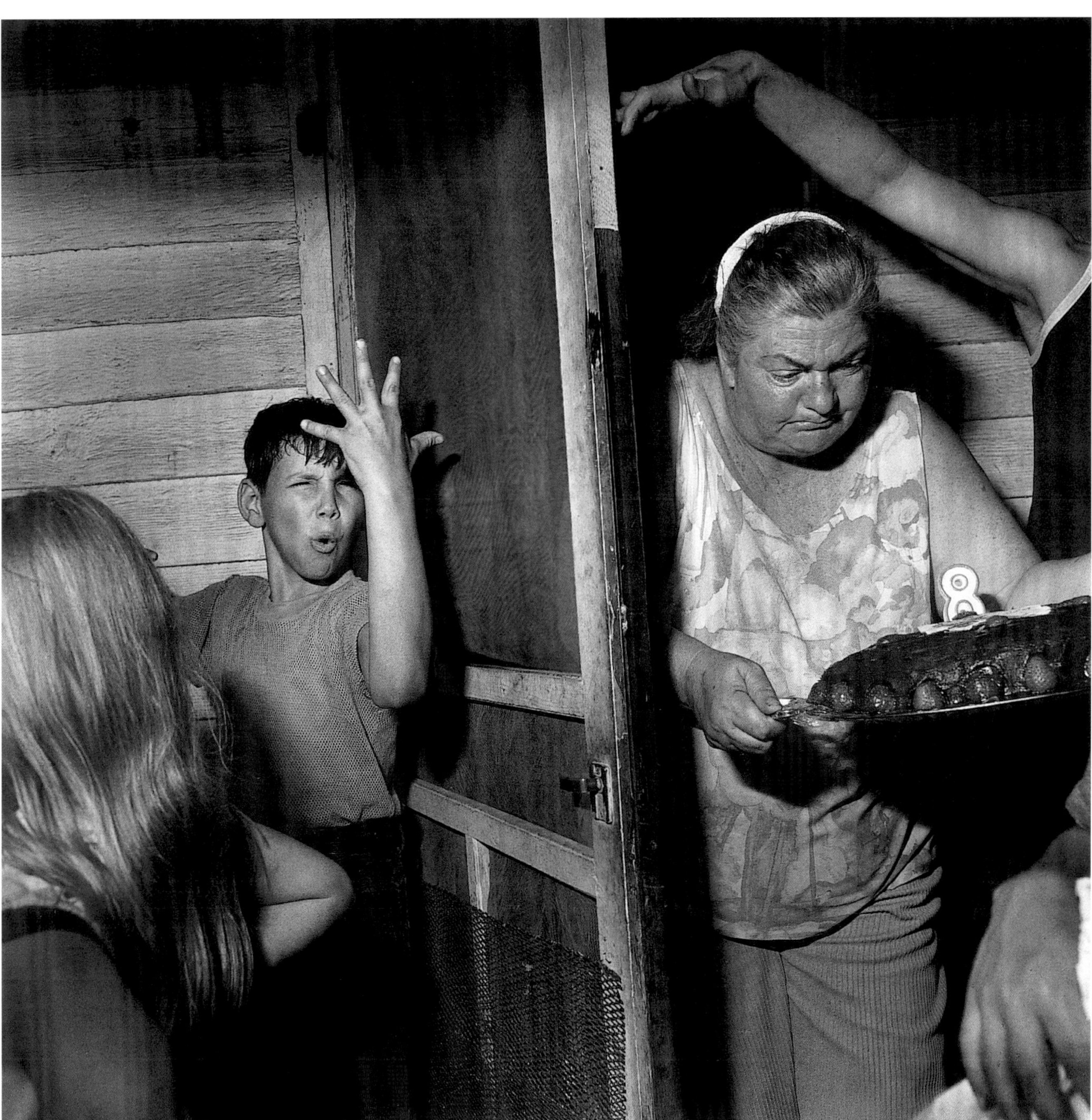

April 1977   Pat Sabatine's Eighth Birthday Party, Martins Creek.

This is one of hundreds of pictures from Martins Creek that couldn't be included in *Social Graces*. Seen from below, sculpted in the twilight with Fink's flash, for the briefest instant this little girl has serendipitously fallen into the pose of Michelangelo's *Dying Slave,* but it is the stopped, kinetic energy of youth that drives this image. Fink often plays with the tension between chaos and order, and here our attention is pushed in three directions at once by the competing glances and movements of the children.

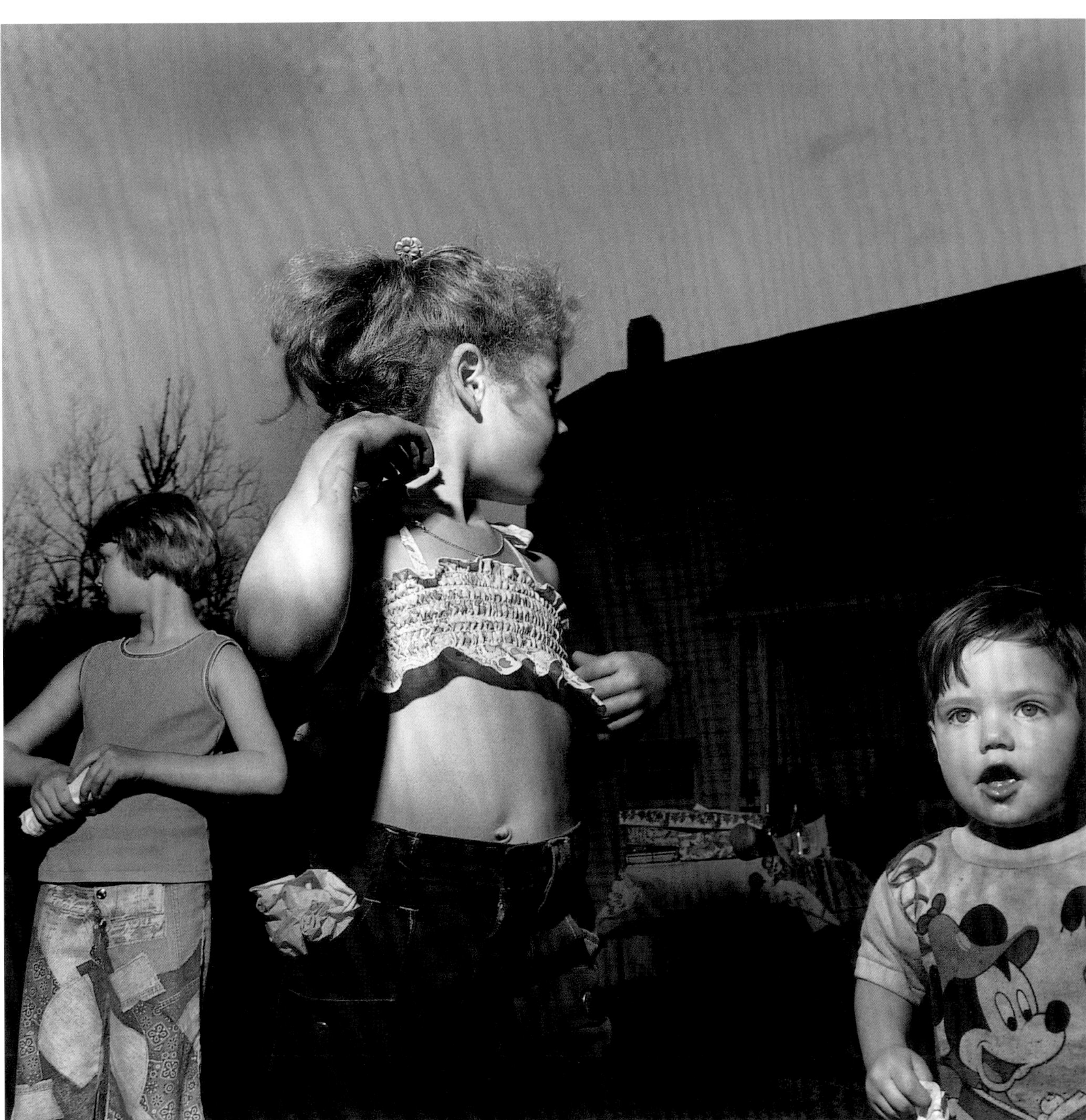

12	June 1977	Oslin's Teen Party, Martins Creek.

This picture would have been filled with visual and emotional interest even without the intertextual captioning provided by the tapestry above the couch. But with the added editorial comment pronounced from on high, irony does battle with utter emotional sincerity. The viewer is forced to reckon with the prospect that, at the moment these teenagers achieve independence from their parents, they guilelessly submit to the enslavement of love and all the complications that go with it.

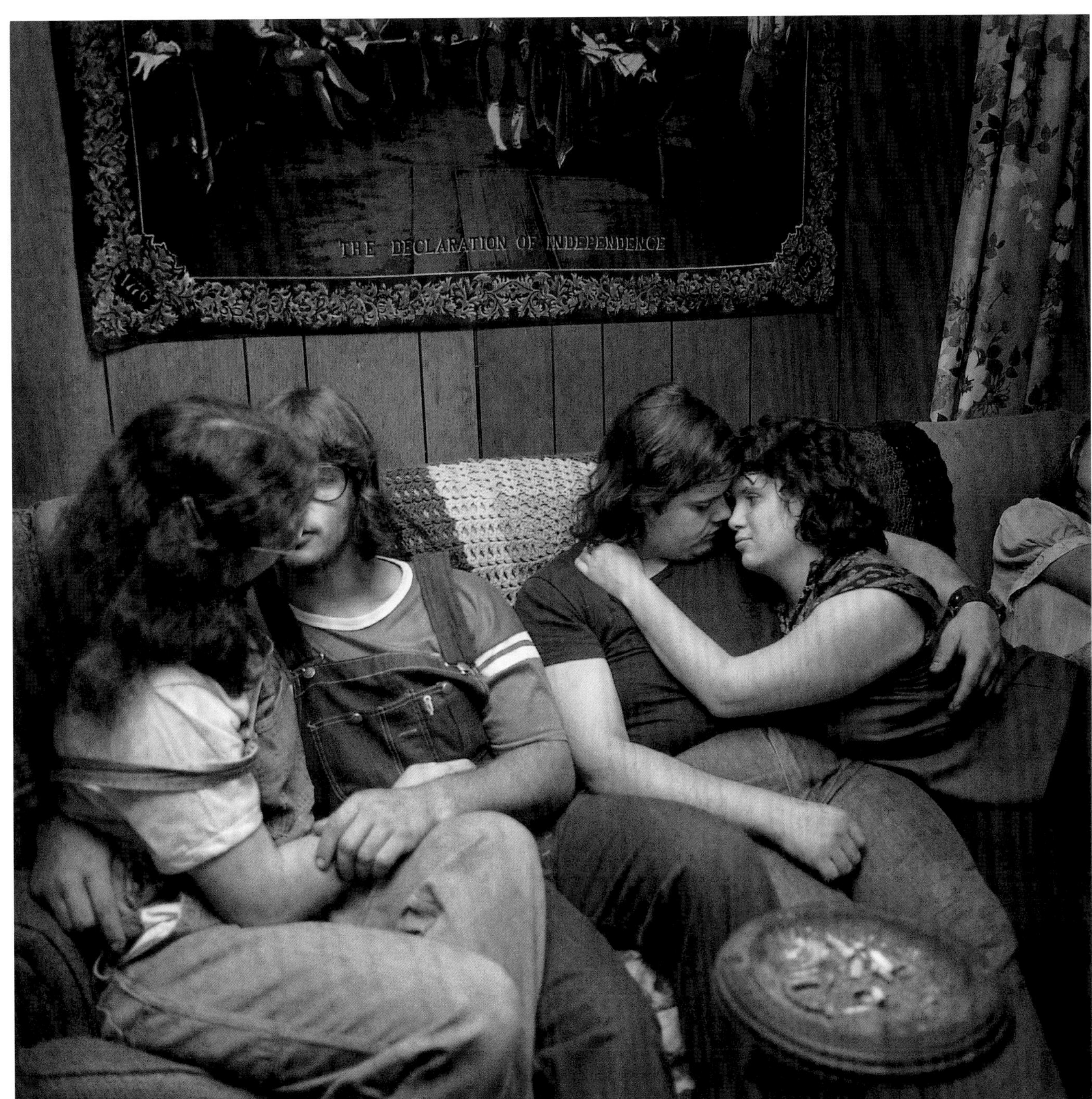

THE DECLARATION OF INDEPENDENCE

January 1979

American Legion, Bangor, Pennsylvania.

Fink truly revels in revelry; he profoundly enjoys depicting the high end of the scale of human emotion. Here, New Year's Eve at the local American Legion hall provides an opportunity to show that life's boisterous pleasures are not exclusively the privilege of the young. The picture builds its emotional weight from the woman's firm embrace of her partner, her ebullient shout, the mirthful expression of the man behind her and the pressing together of bodies in a collective celebration of the future.

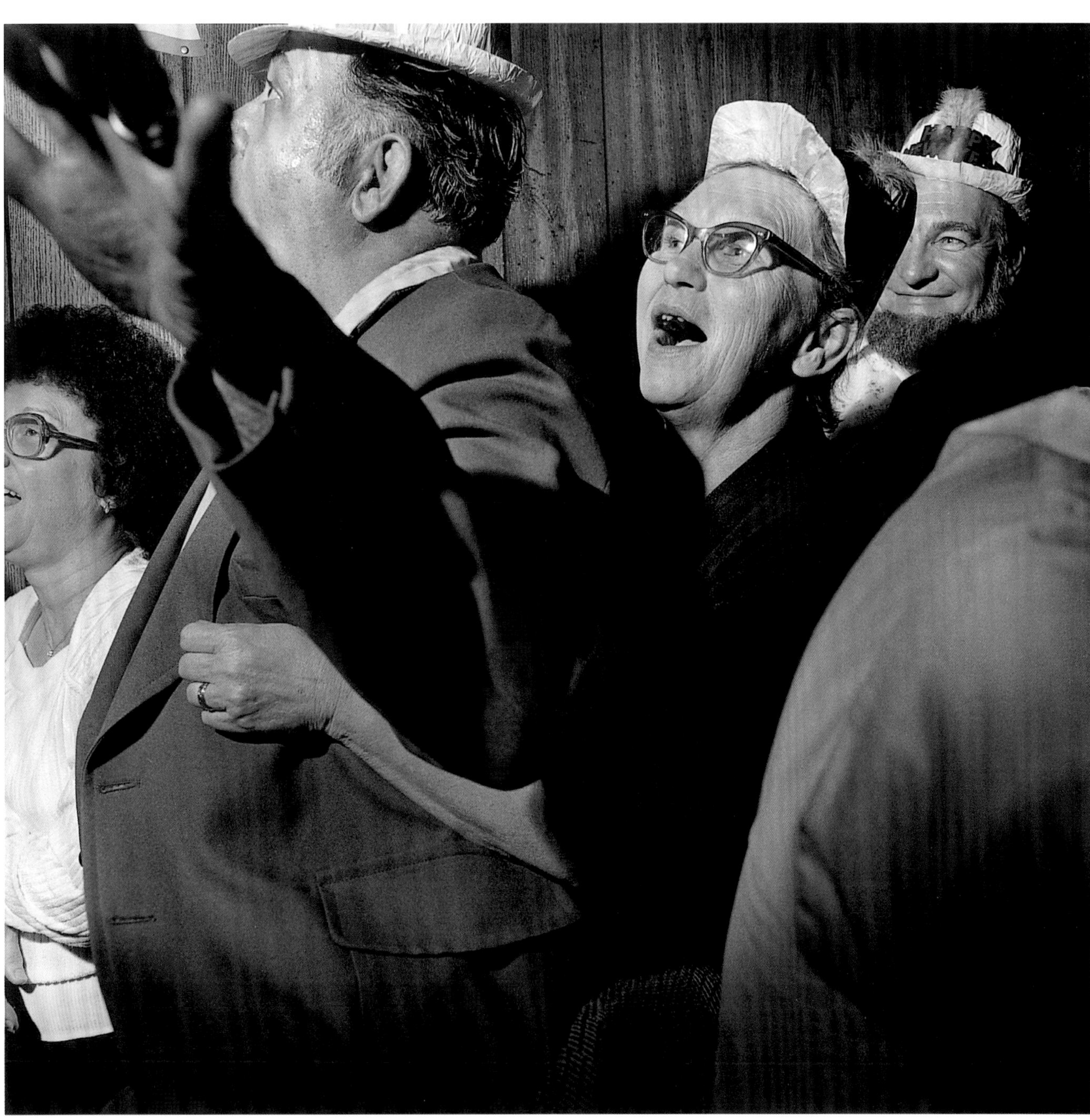

14

August 1979   Allentown Fair, Pennsylvania.

Always on the lookout for the 'raw, sensual motor', Fink recognizes the fraught embrace of a teenage couple near the sideshows at the county fair. The flash catches their antipodal expressions – joyfully open and darkly self-conscious – as an enigmatic carnival landscape falls away behind them. We might be further tempted to read the signs in the background as a serendipitous commentary upon the principal actors, as in the dog-like behaviour of a young man on the make or the waffling of a young girl who can't decide.

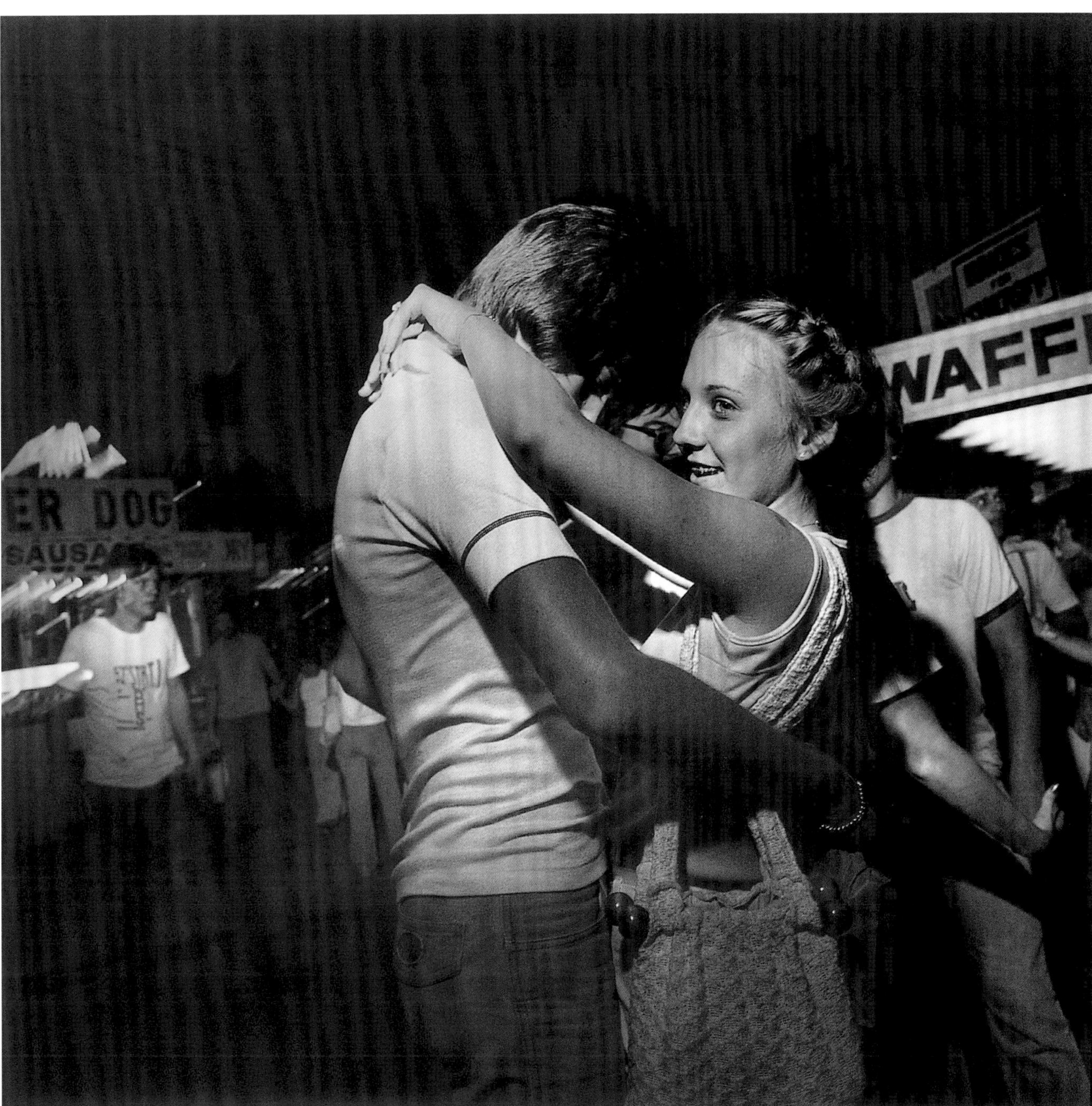
ER DOG
SAUSA
WAFF

15

September 1979

Praying Mantis, Martins Creek.

Born and bred in the city, Fink became a committed gardener when he moved to his farm in Pennsylvania. He took a break from taking photographs of the black-tie parties one summer to work on projects at home. Here, he shifts scale from human to insect society, getting down on all fours with a macro-lens to photograph the praying mantises he imported to control the undesirables of the garden. With the camera's very shallow depth of field, the praying mantis emerges as if out of a fog, gazing with anthropomorphic curiosity at the vertically configured 'eyes' of the Rolleiflex's twin lenses.

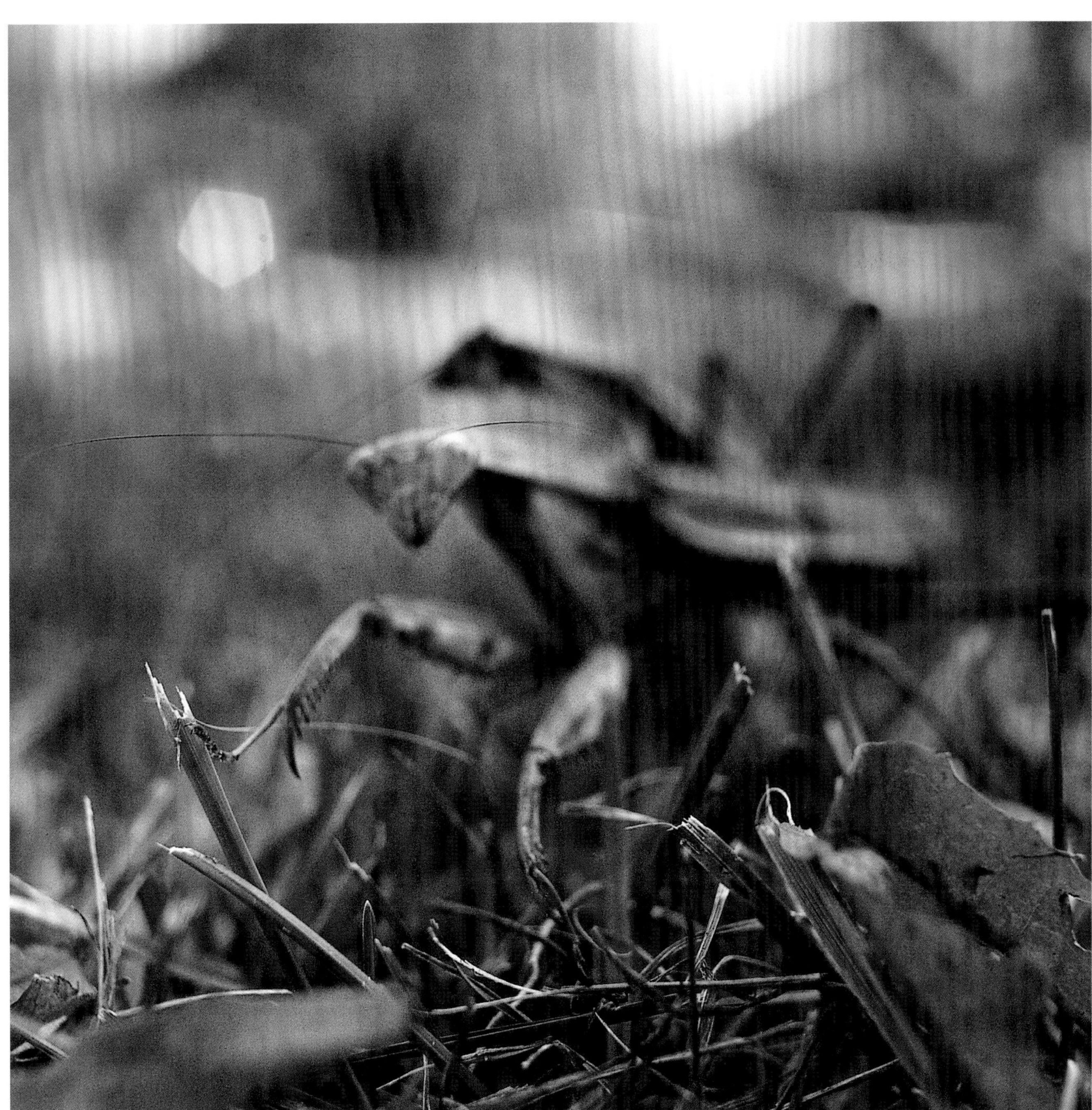

   October 1979   Praying Mantis, Martins Creek.

This image tests the mantis's powers of mimesis: its ability to be mistaken for a stalk of grass. With photography's superior powers of vision and its ability to record minute differences in surface and texture, we immediately spy the mantis dangling drolly from the top centre of the frame.

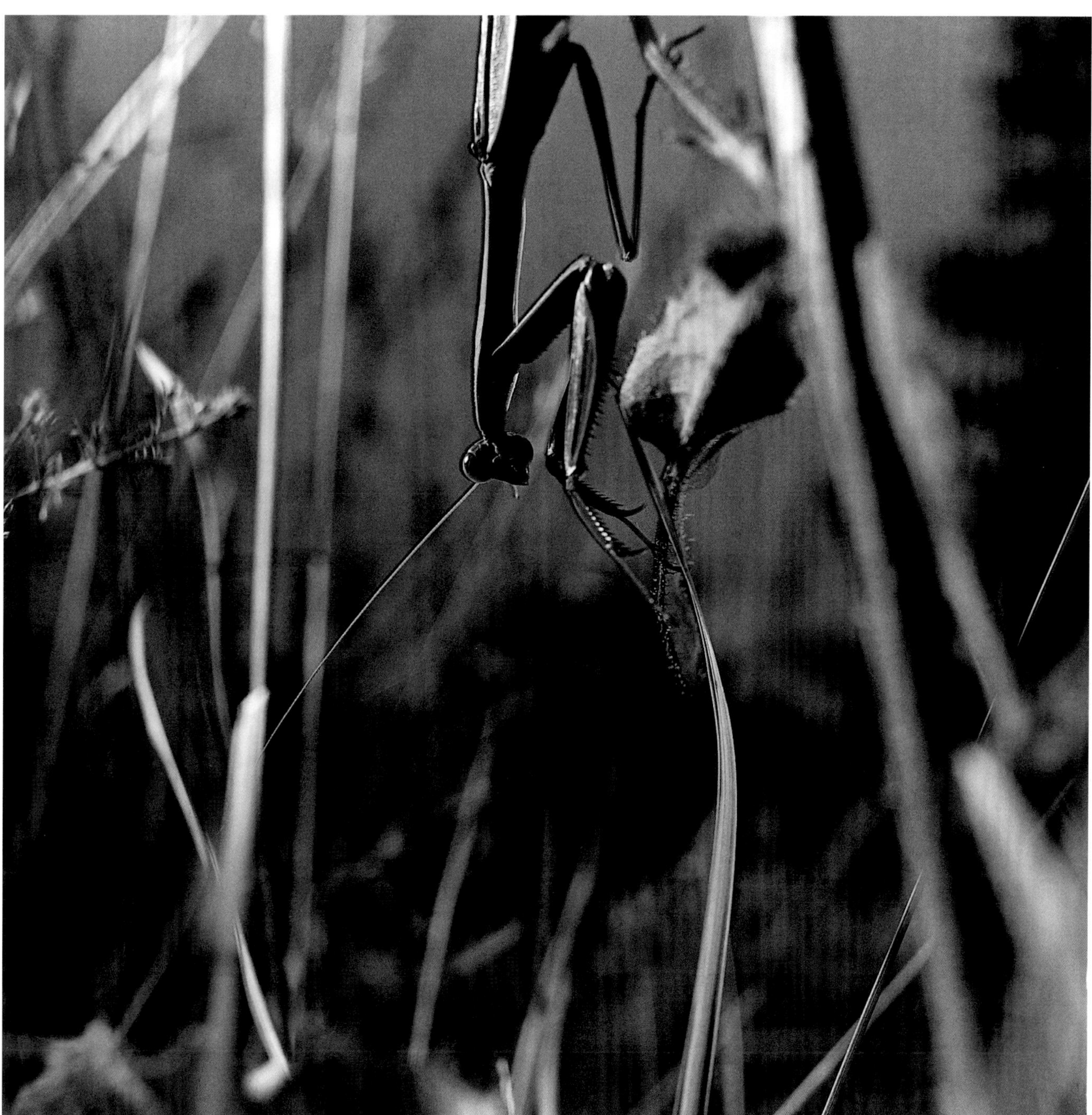

17

1980   Thanksgiving, Martins Creek.

Four people look directly at Fink's lens in this portrait made at a Fink Thanksgiving dinner, but it is the absolutely steady, knowing gaze exchanged between Larry and his mother, anchoring the centre of the photographic frame, that hierarchically orders everything else in the picture. It would be difficult to overemphasize the importance Sylvia Fink had in her son's life. Describing her as 'the most radical, charismatic, exquisitely magnetic, unbelievably controlling, insecure, absolutely oversecure, most complex character that you've ever seen', Fink recognizes Sylvia's genetic legacy in his own intense will and drive.

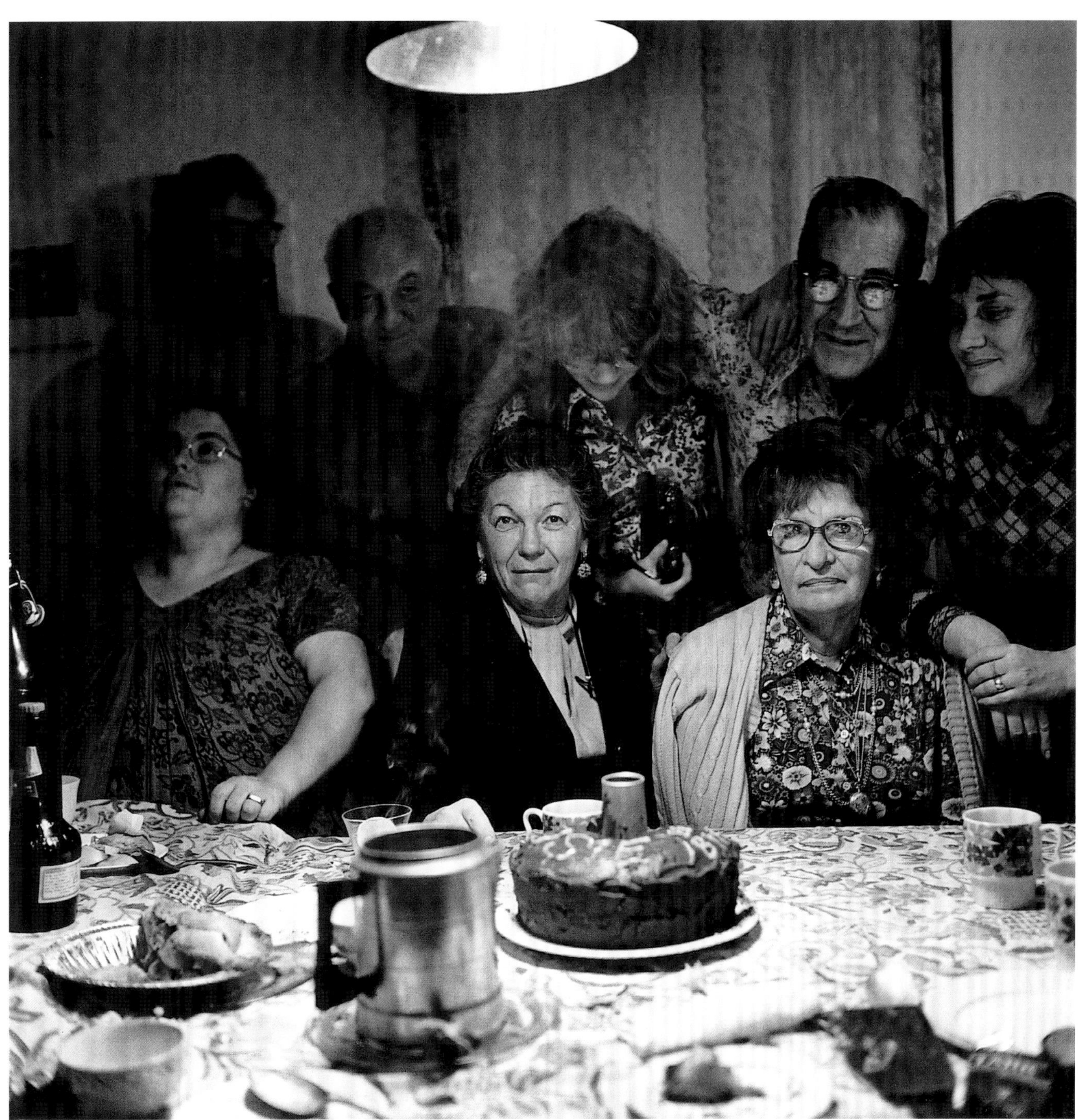

18

October 1982   Self-portrait with Molly, Martins Creek.

Fink's personal history as a male surrounded by powerful females continues in his relationship with Molly, his daughter. In this photograph Molly, minimally assisted by her father, points imperiously at the camera, as if commanding the exposure. The resultant image might be called a collaborative double self-portrait.

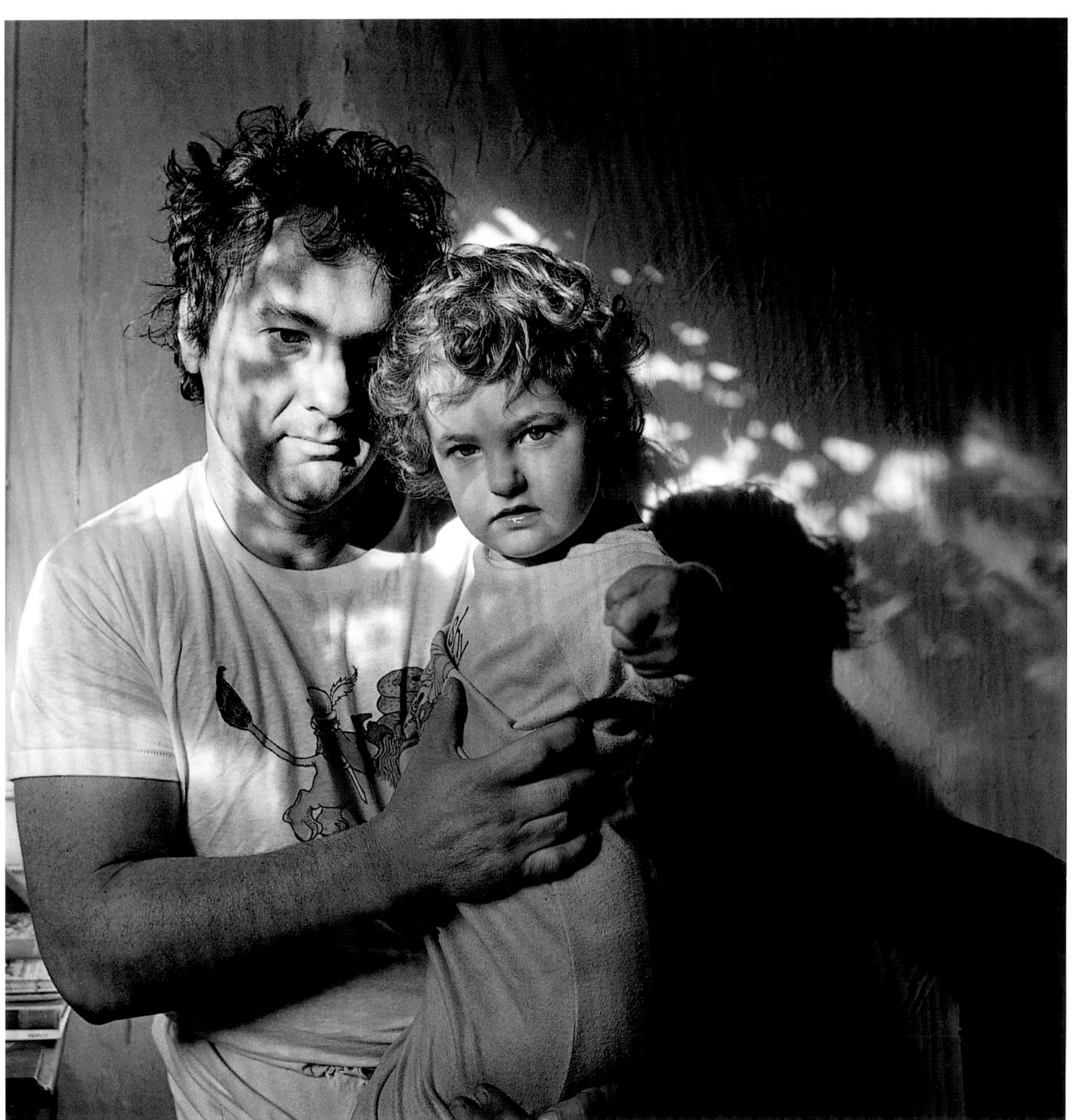

19

April 1988   Sylvia Kleinman and Maggie Keuhn, Philadelphia.

Photographing his mother and her close friend, Fink found the strength of their intimacy manifested in the gesture of their firmly clasped hands. Maggie's inward gaze, directed at nothing in particular but nevertheless reflecting profound happiness, stands in contrast to Sylvia's equivocal outward gaze, which conveys a sense of knowing sadness.

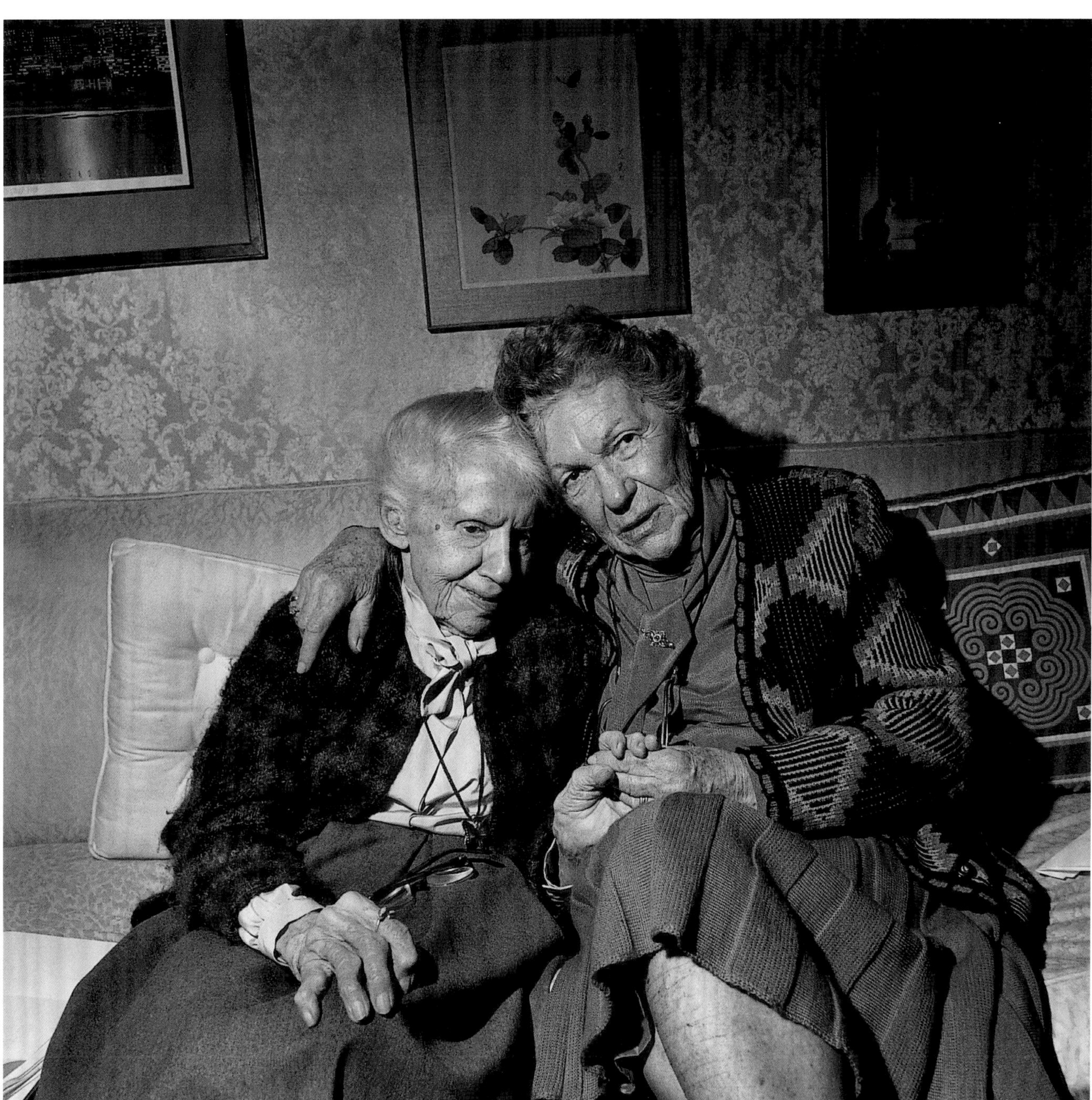

20

July 1988

Côte d'Azur, France.

On assignment for the magazine Condé Nast *Traveller,* Fink spent an afternoon at the Côte d'Azur villa of this nonagenarian. Once she and her twin sister had ruled the social world of the Riviera, but now her society consisted of servants and two 'secretly manipulative, but adoring' caretakers. The indeterminate light – is it day, night, or twilight? – underscores her liminal stage of life. Her caretaker, peering down from the upper-right corner, may be all that keeps her tethered to the present.

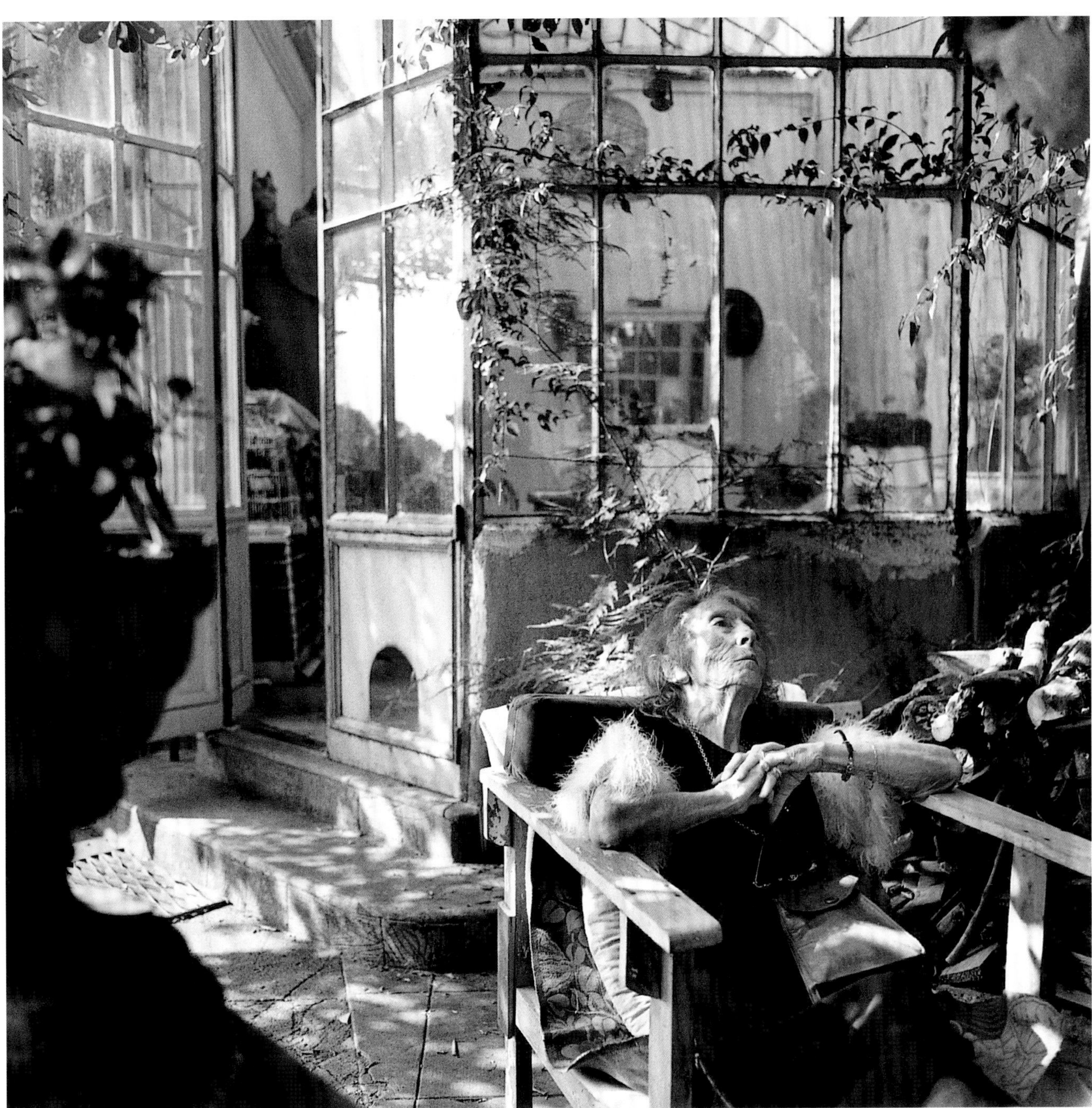

21

September 1989   Ventozelo Farm, Ervedosa do Douro, Portugal.

As a photographer who has always been more interested in culture than nature (unless one includes what we call 'human nature'), Fink is not known for his landscapes. Commissioned to photograph the grape harvest in Portugal, the beautifully lush, terraced river valley impressed him, but here the landscape still forms the backdrop to the greater drama of human activities. Fink followed harvesters as they worked their way down the hillside vineyard. The muscular body of a boy, seen from behind, subtly bends in accord with the undulating terrain.

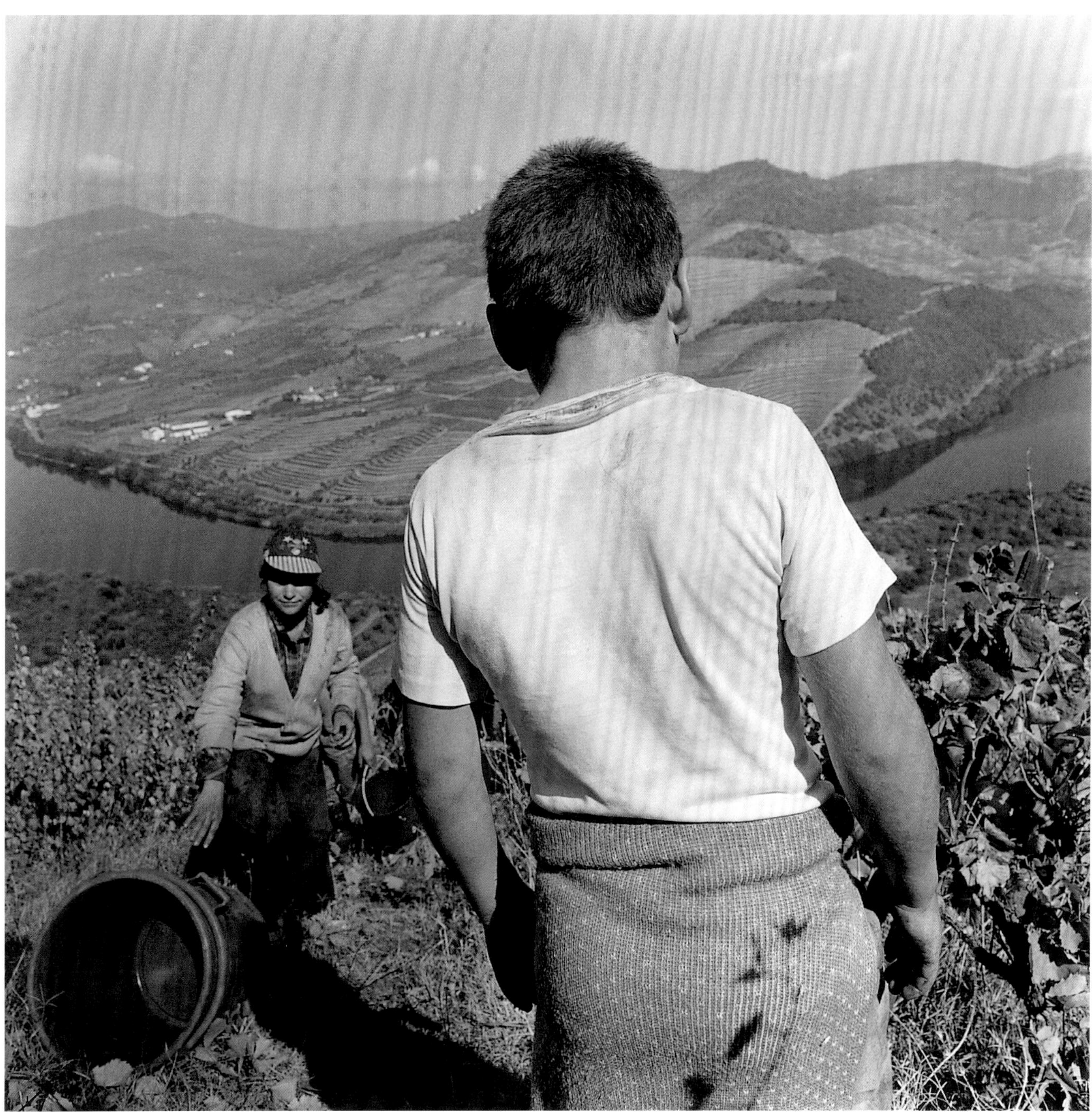

22

September 1989   Ventozelo Farm, Ervedosa do Douro, Portugal.

In Portugal, Fink photographed reputedly the last commercial vintner using traditional human methods for crushing grapes. For this picture he used a horizontal format to give a wider view of the low-tech vat with its human workers. The photographic medium grants the utmost tactility to the sticky, glistening, viscous materiality of the crushed grapes.

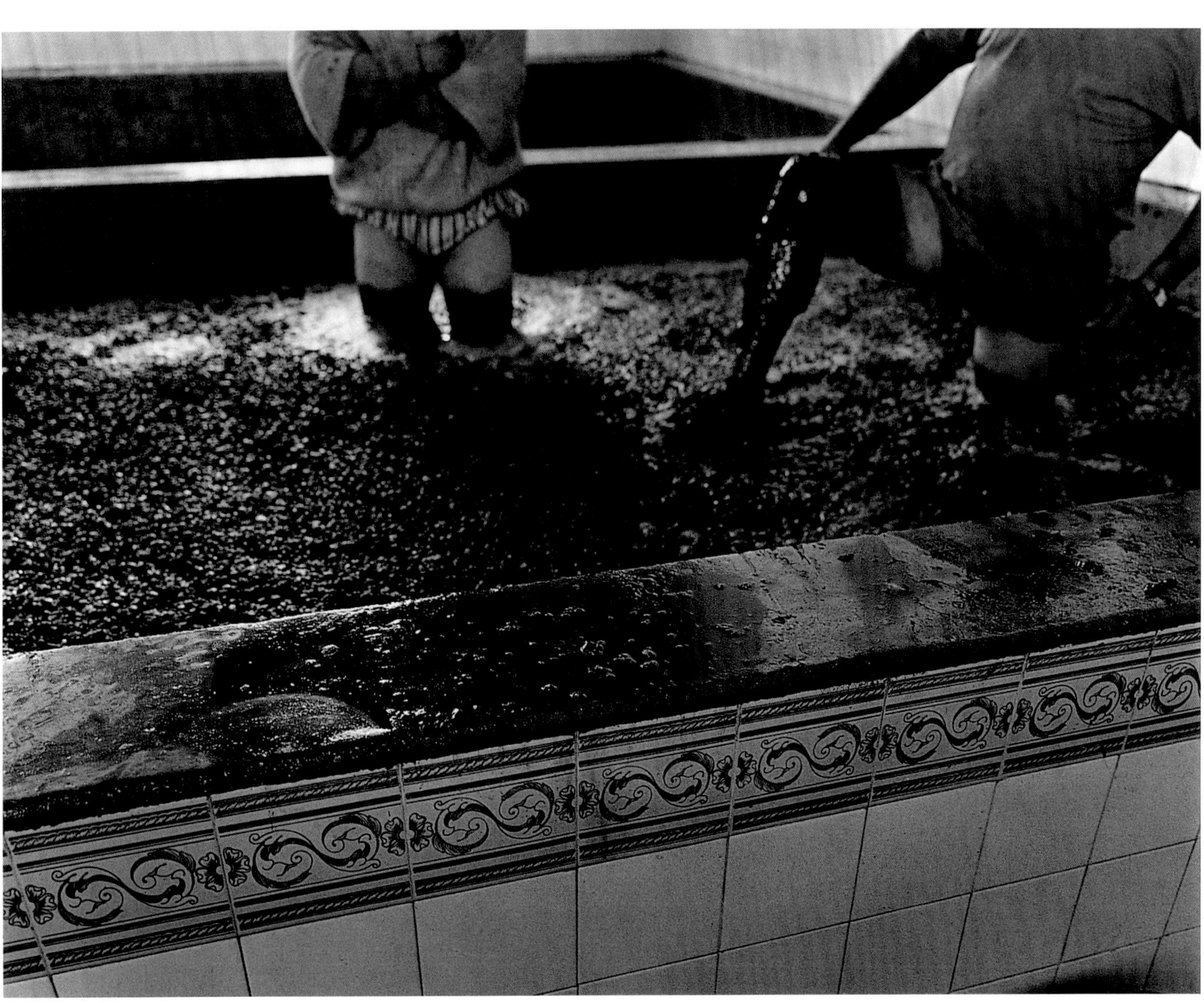

23

October 1989 | Bear Sterns, Wall Street, New York City.

The uniformity of these Wall Street stockbrokers, with their identical haircuts, racial profile and crisp white shirts, suggests their monotonous, corporate interchangeability, or makes it possible to see them as conjoined twins: a single super-broker, bearish and bullish at the same time.

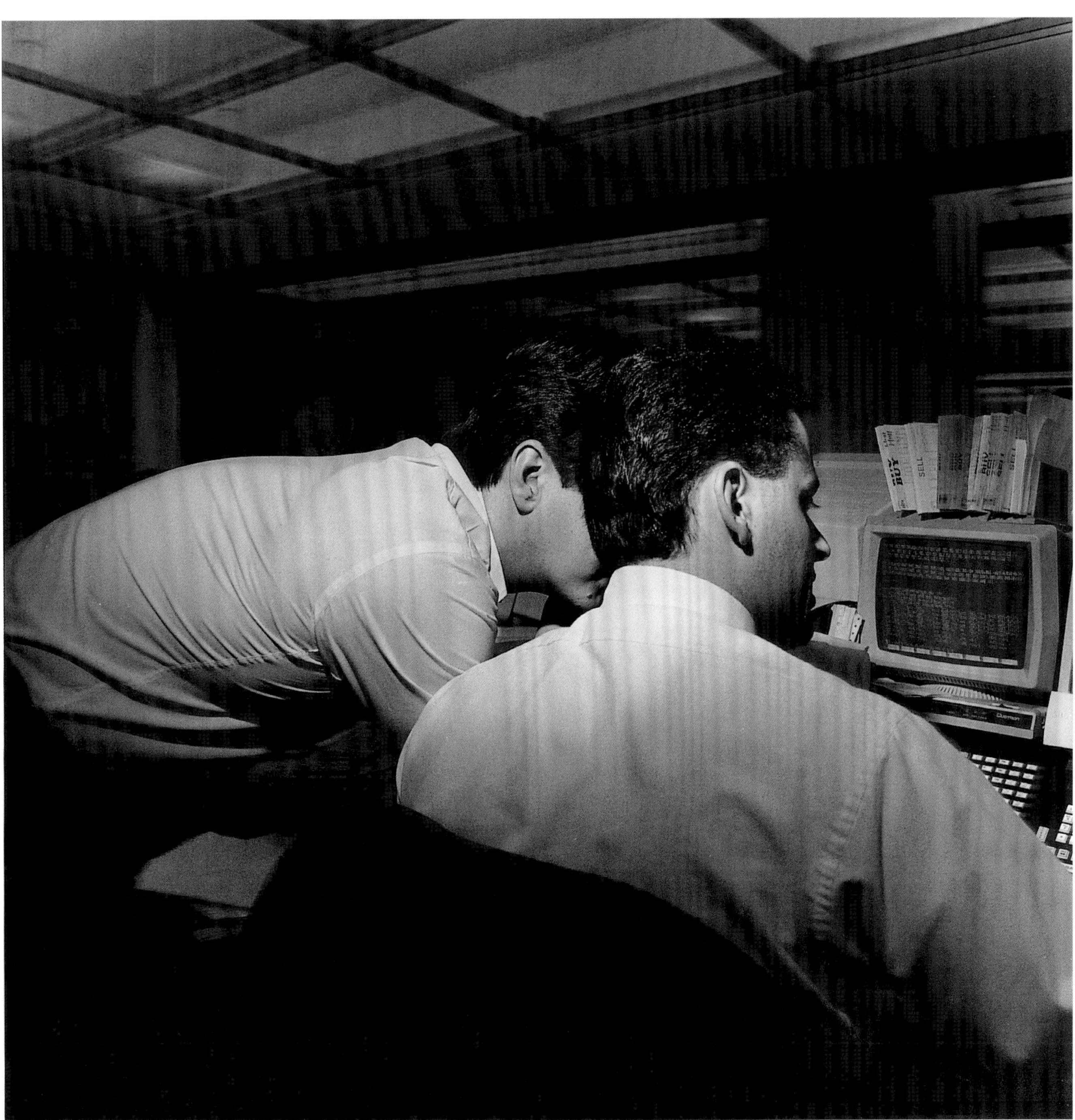

October 1989

Wall Street, New York City.

Almost as if he were haunting Hanover Square – a famous drinking destination for brokers – Fink stood watching passers-by from the subway steps. Although the viewer cannot know this man's circumstances, in this context one nevertheless concludes that the man's intense capitalist drive has left him unsettled and bitter.

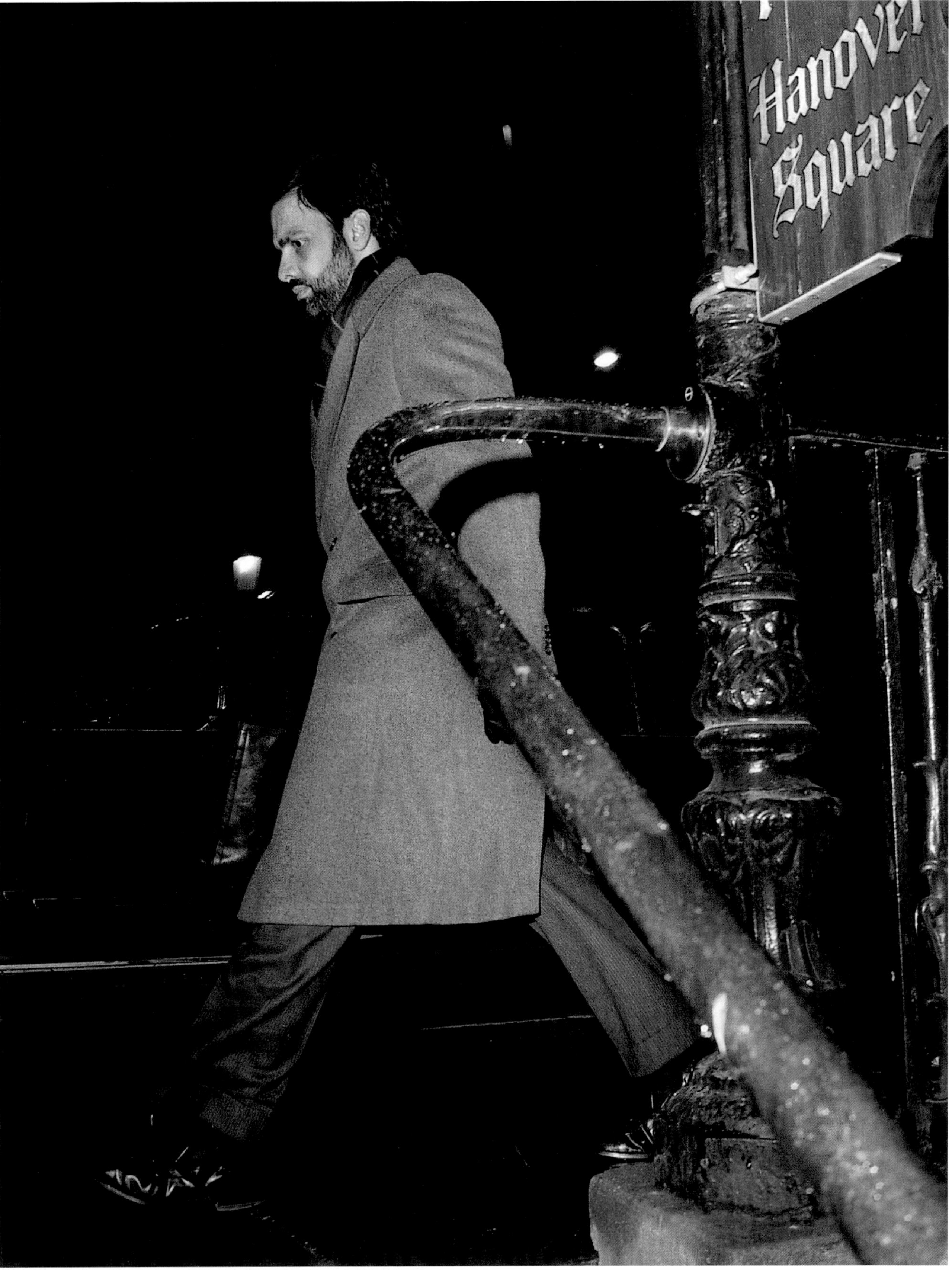
Hanover
Square

25

October 1992 | Toricelli-Zimmer Campaign, New Jersey.

This picture is part of a group Fink ironically calls his 'White Power' series – images of the corporate and institutional power in America that overwhelmingly rests in the hands of white leaders. Fink's flash adds ominous shadows to the flat, fluorescent light of this drab campaign 'war room' and heightens the air of banal conspiracy. The strategy diagram on the blackboard draws an amusing parallel with the pro-football locker room, but the team-mates' collective lack of vigour raises questions as to who is fit to carry the ball.

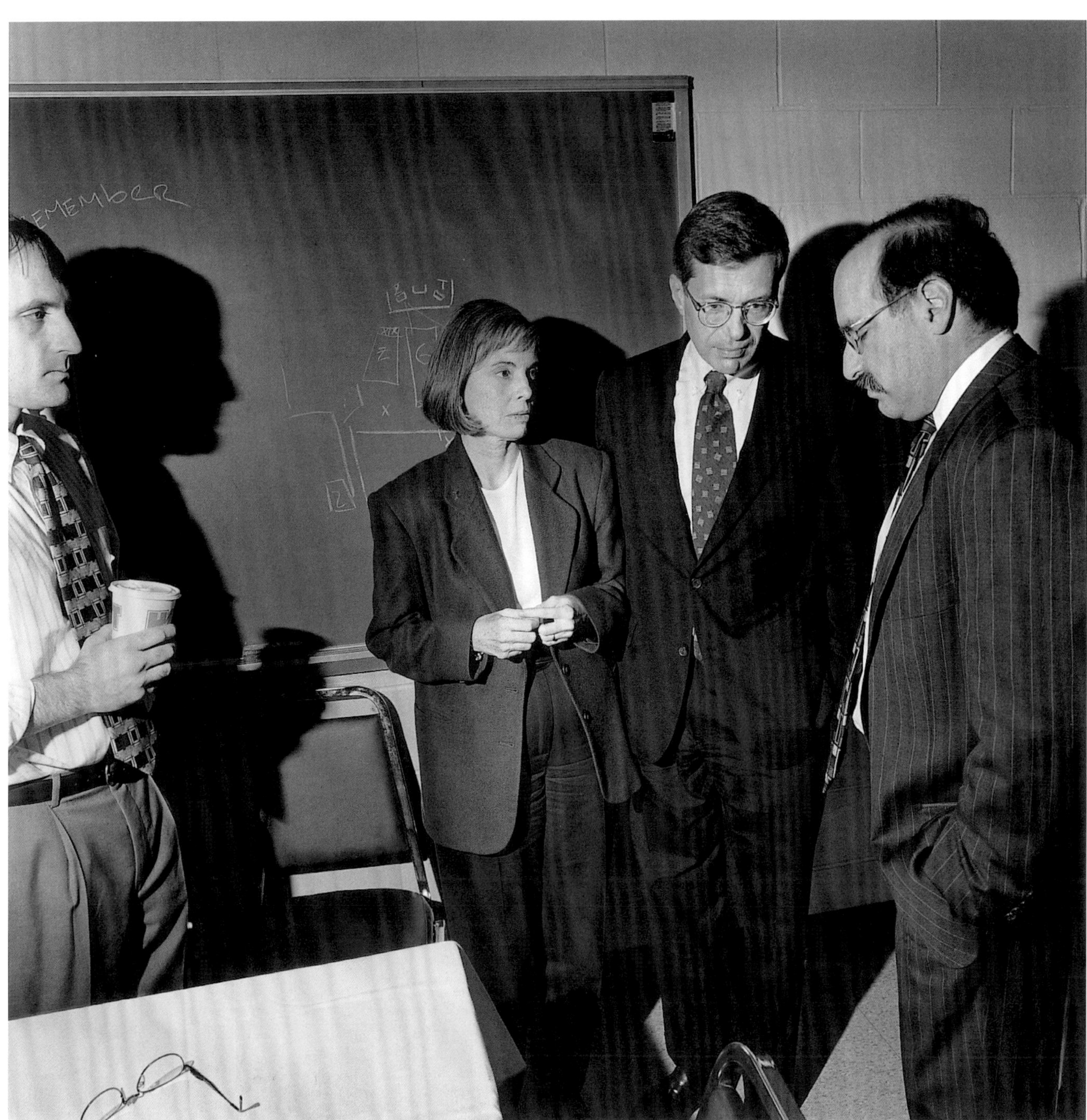

26

November 1992   Ralph Reed, Christian Coalition, the Religious Right, Washington, DC.

Fink delights in miniaturizing the powerful and he is more than adept
at finding the interesting picture, even in the most controlled situations.
This has led to many assignments covering political campaigns. Here
Ralph Reed, a charismatic leader of the religious right, enters the stage
at a national convention. He is dwarfed by his own rhetoric, the symbols
of his campaign: an American flag and the surprisingly secular, even
corporate, logo of the Christian Coalition.

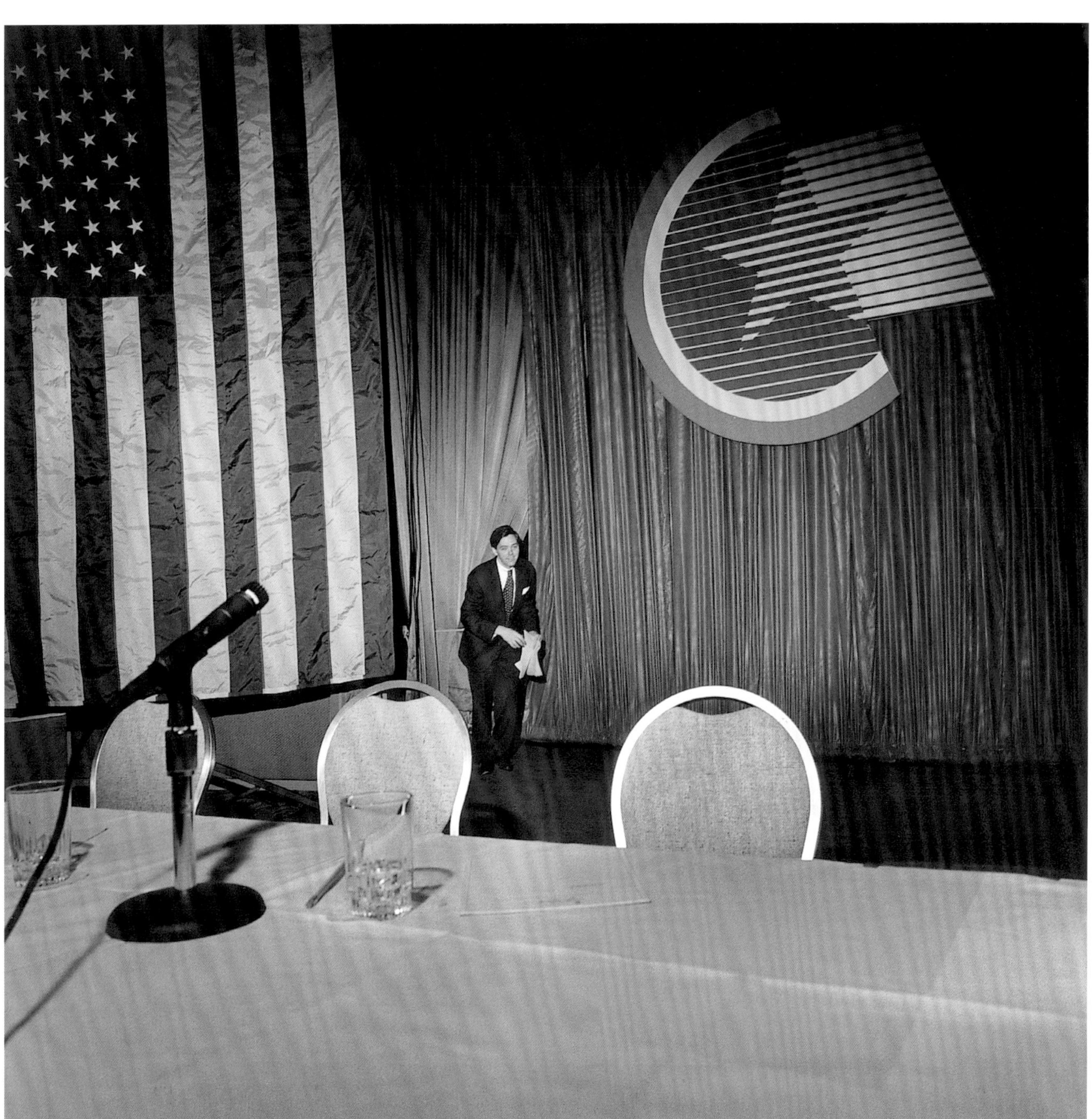

Improper advancement of the film double-exposed several pictures on a roll taken at a convention of the Christian Coalition. Fink liked the result for its repetition of forms and its skewering view of a blandly devoted supporter who nevertheless appears to leap from his seat, doubling himself in what might be termed the applause of lukewarm enthusiasm.

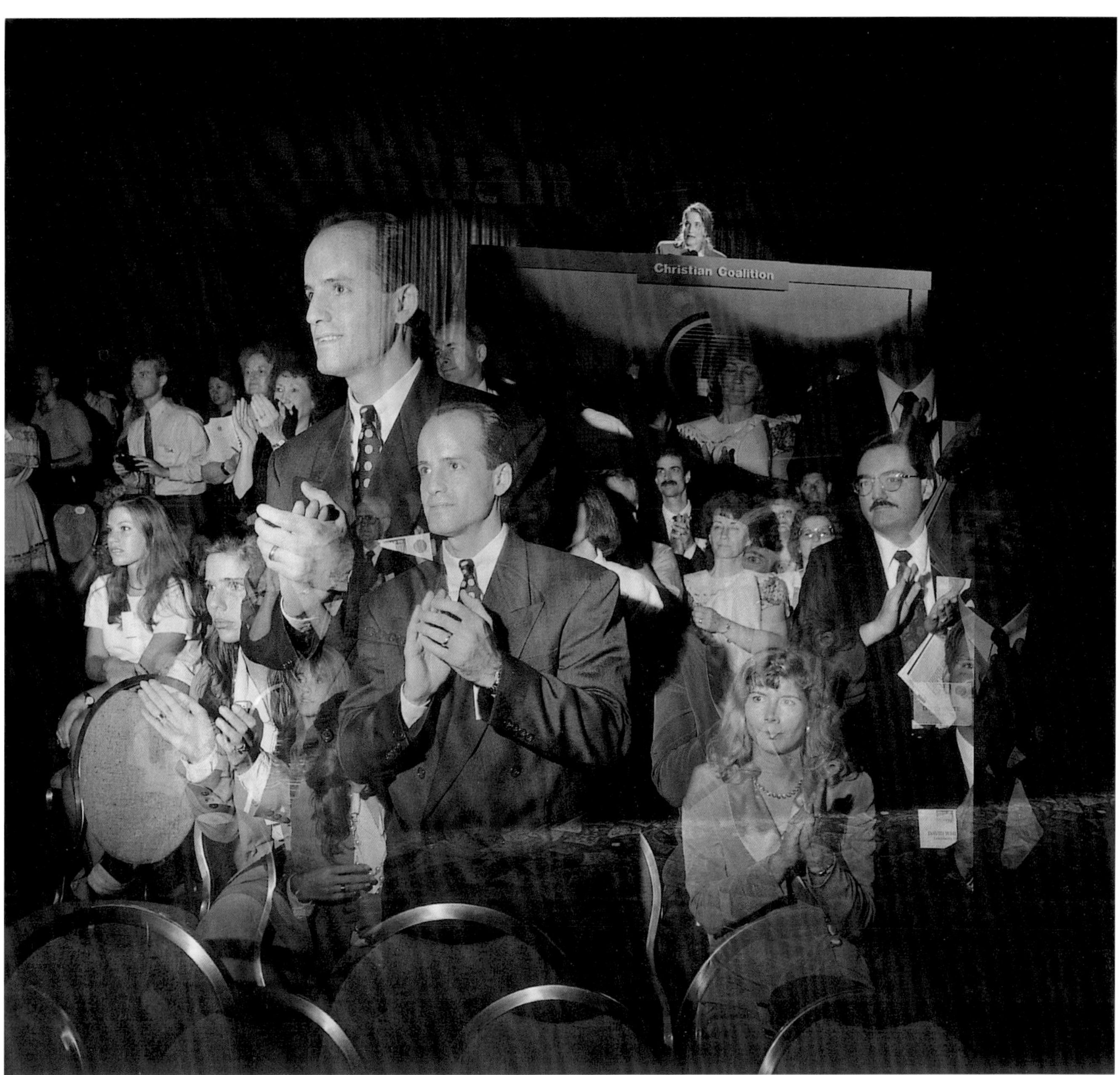
Christian Coalition

November 1992

Ralph Reed, Christian Coalition, the Religious Right, Washington, DC.

Fink, who often describes himself as an old-school Marxist humanist,
engages in more political satire in photographing a book-signing at a
convention of the religious right. This hallucinatory double-exposure
projects a ghostly image of money changing hands beneath the phallic
extension of a microphone. The neo-conservative figureheads who mouth
the words that drive their money machine are caught, paparazzi-style,
in mid-blink and mid-utterance, grasping and gasping.

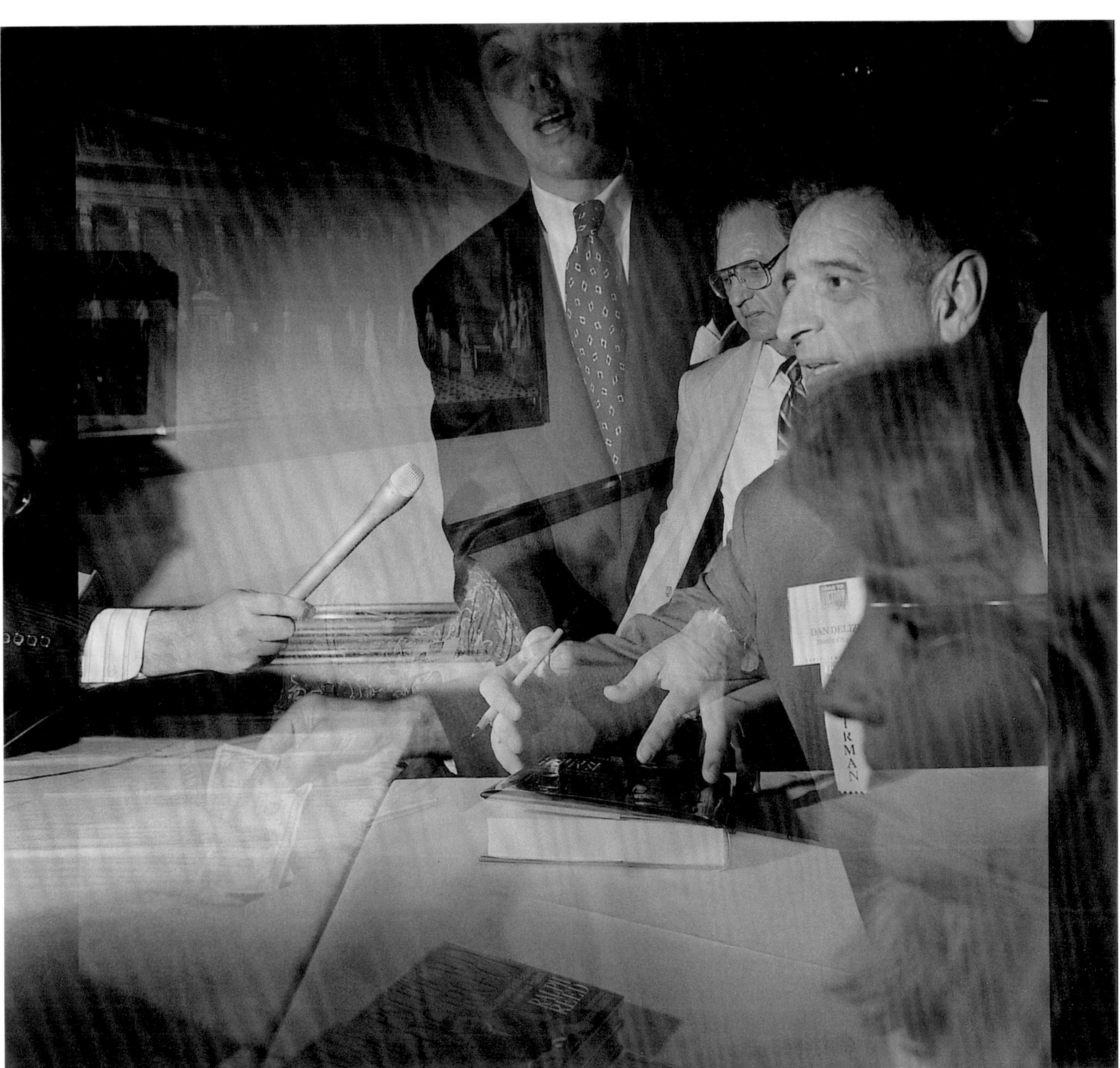

29

December 1992   Morgan Fairchild and Tom Hayden, Political Consortium, Atlanta, Georgia.

This photograph, showing politician Tom Hayden towering masterfully over the glamour queen Morgan Fairchild, opens up the discourse of male–female relations, highlighting issues of sex, power and dominance. Their respective uniforms of hyperfemininity and hypermasculinity, together with their body language, offer ample material for deconstructing the codes of gender. A critique, yes, but the photographer's ambiguous place in all this should not be overlooked, just as Fink could not overlook the view afforded by Fairchild's neckline.

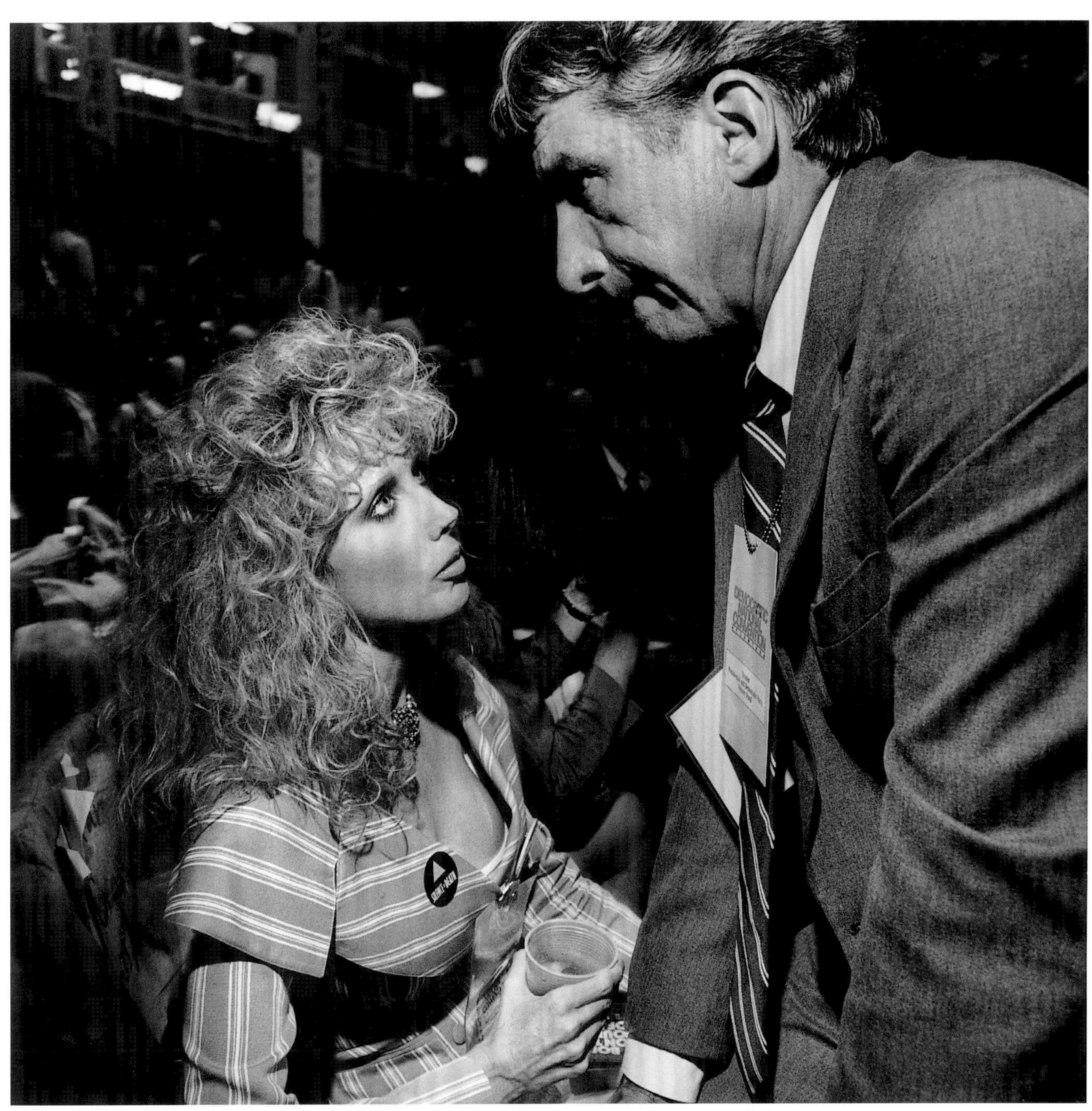

30

January 1993 | Boxing, Blue Horizon, Philadelphia, Pennsylvania.

Fink's parents were boxing enthusiasts, and Fink himself took an early interest in the sport, although when the fight broadcasts moved from radio to television, he found the spectacle made him too anxious to watch. To his surprise, when asked to cover a story about the young Mike Tyson and his manager, then working out of a gym in upstate New York, he discovered that being ringside put him instantly at ease. Since then he has spent many hours in the gym, taking in the wider culture of boxing and its aspirants. With its discomforting incongruities, this image takes on a surrealist flavour: the arrested violence of the blow, the headless figure and the massive, erect figure of the bandaged boxing dummy.

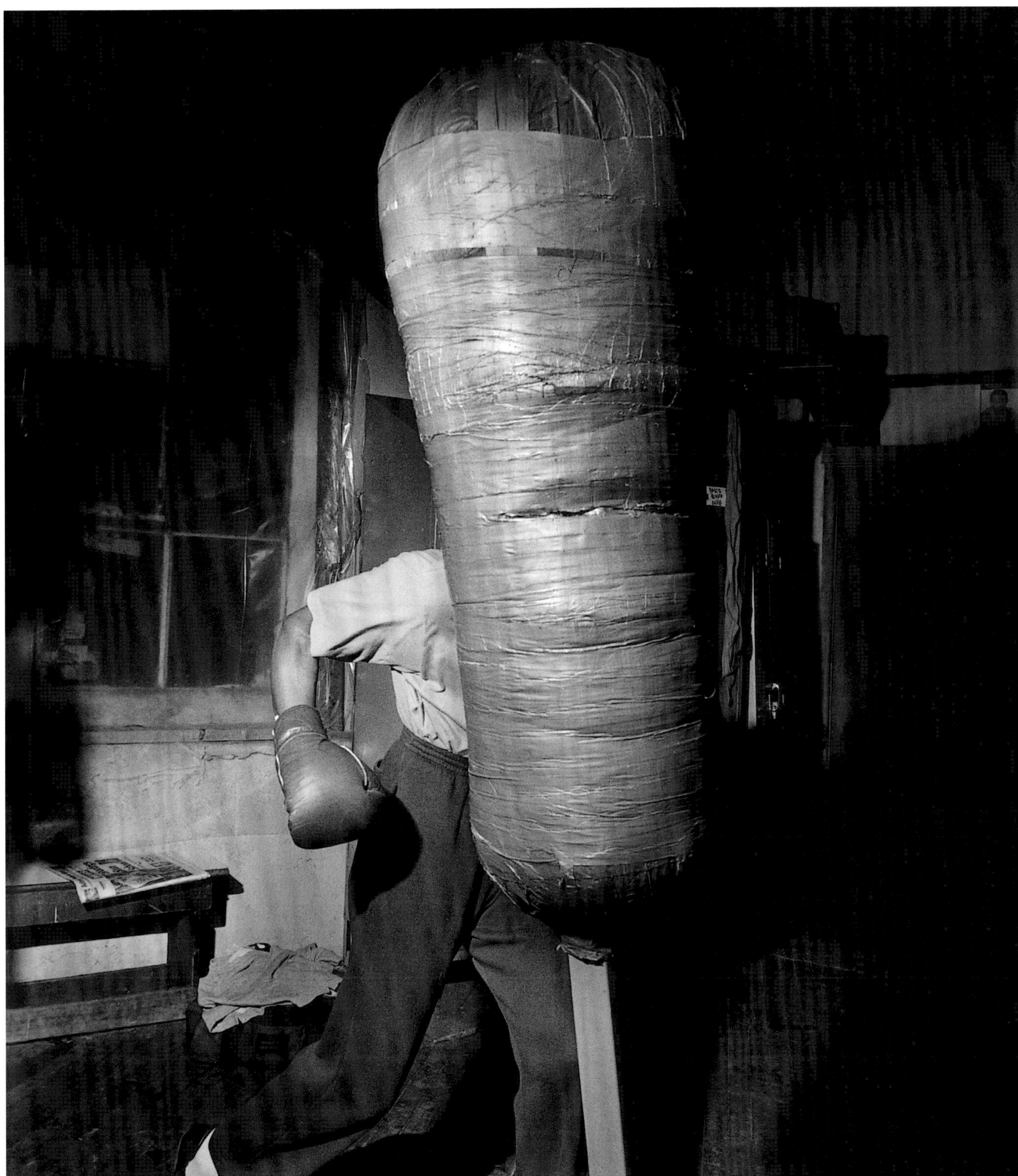

31

January 1993 | Boxing, Champs Gym, Philadelphia, Pennsylvania.

With its union of physicality and psychology, boxing became a natural photographic obsession for Fink. Part of his interest in the sport lies in its being a traditional medium of black aspiration for success and recognition, hence his preference for small, inner-city gyms and the regional boxing culture. What he found there was an 'amazing combination of innocence and power, both in body and mind.'

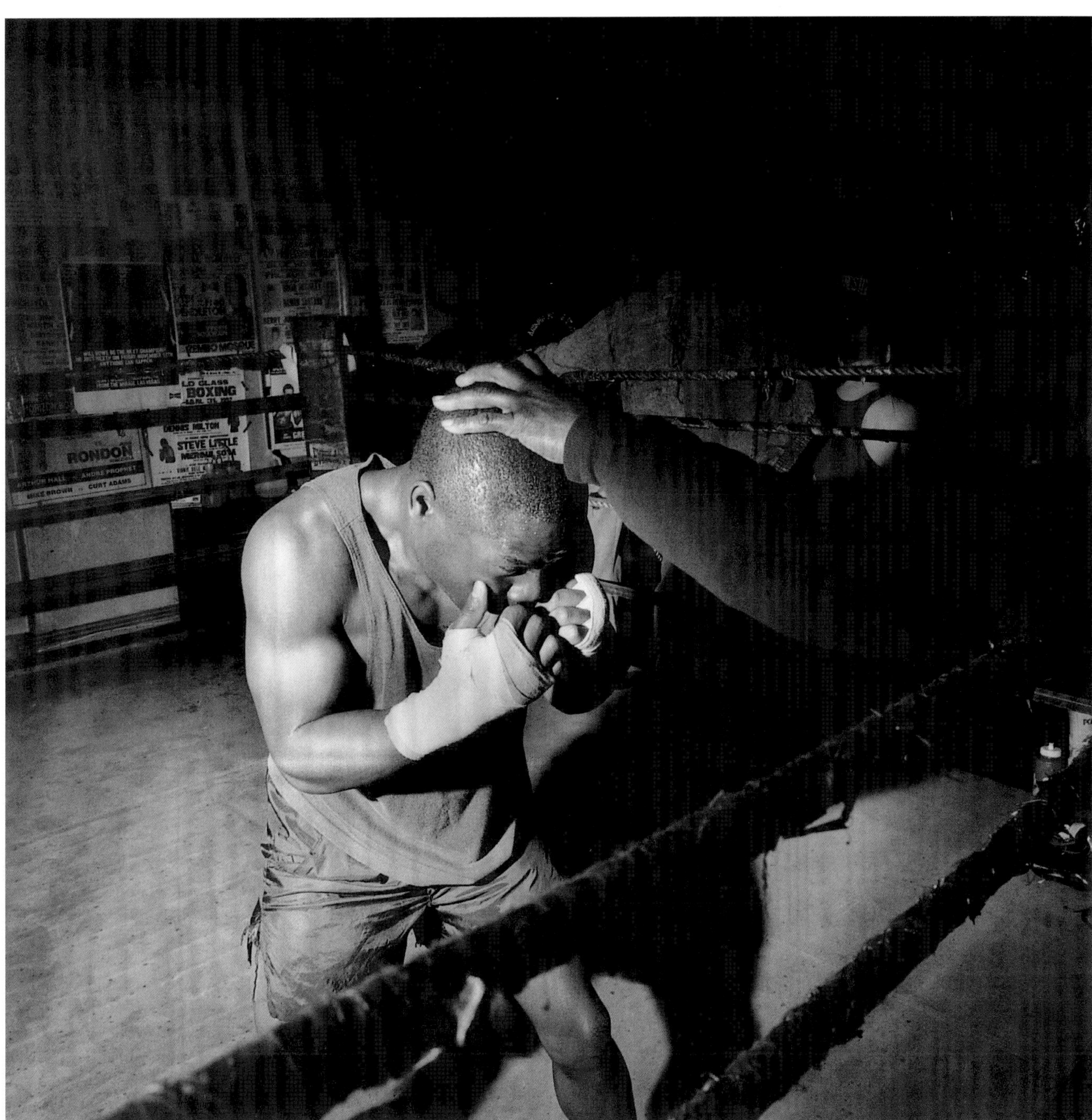
LO CLASS
BOXING
RONDON
ANDRE PROPHET
MIKE BROWN vs CURT ADAMS
DENNIS MILTON
STEVE LITTLE

January 1993

Boxing, Blue Horizon, Philadelphia, Pennsylvania.

This may be Fink's most purely distilled portrait. Nothing is shown but the boxer's face and shoulders, but what we see is a man in a profoundly altered and utterly private state of mind, fresh from the physical and psychological rush of the fight.

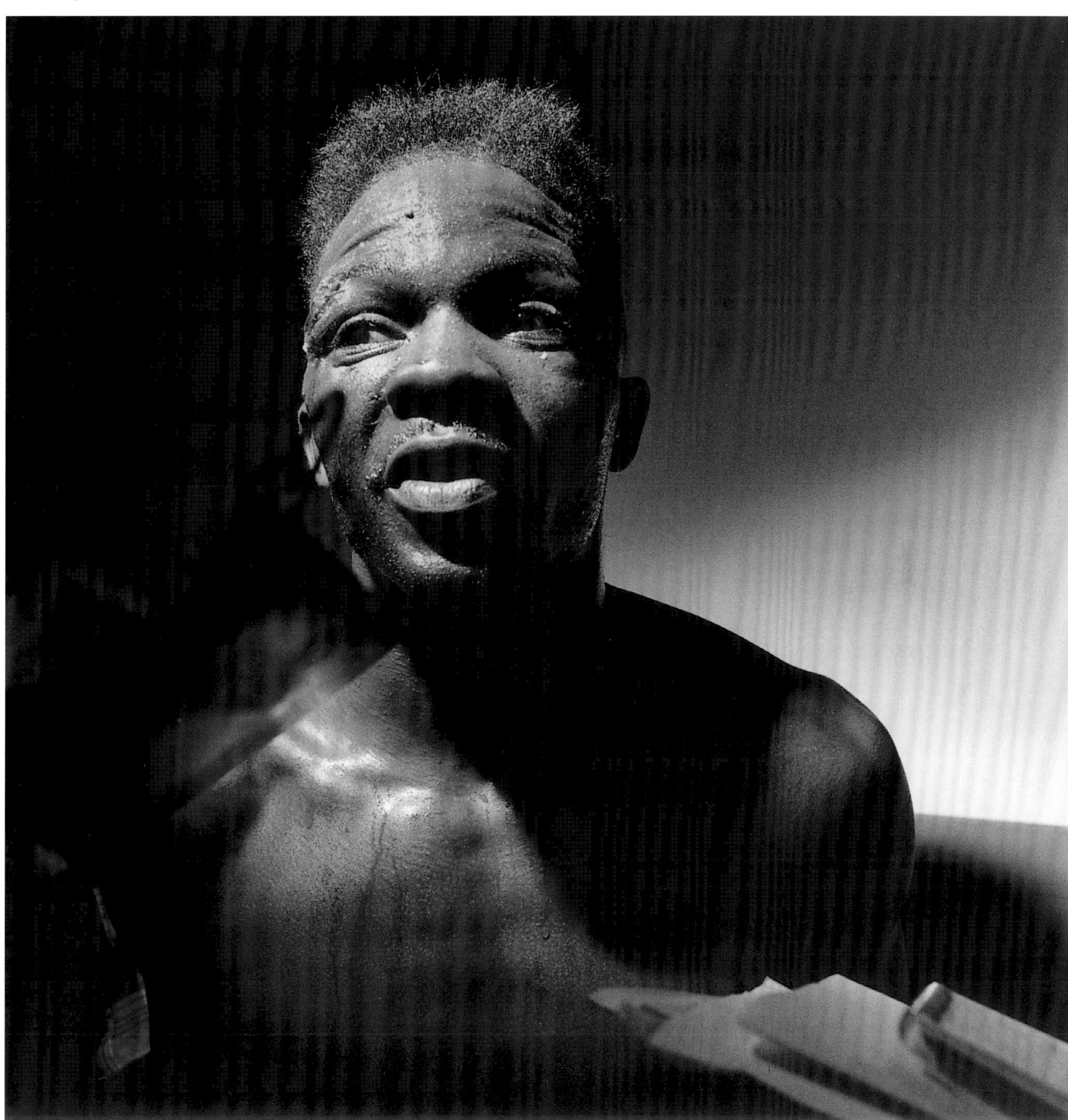

December 1994 | Boxing, Blue Horizon, Philadelphia, Pennsylvania.

Fink recalls the old days of boxing when the sport was openly political, a territory that ethnic groups strove to conquer and defend. This luminous portrait, used as the cover image for Fink's *Boxing* (1997), evokes some of that residual pride. The luscious line and texture of the black satin hood, the power of the glistening jaw, the beatific expression of the mouth, confer an air of heroism and accomplishment on this unknown boxer and create a symbolic negation of the image of a hooded Ku Klux Klansman.

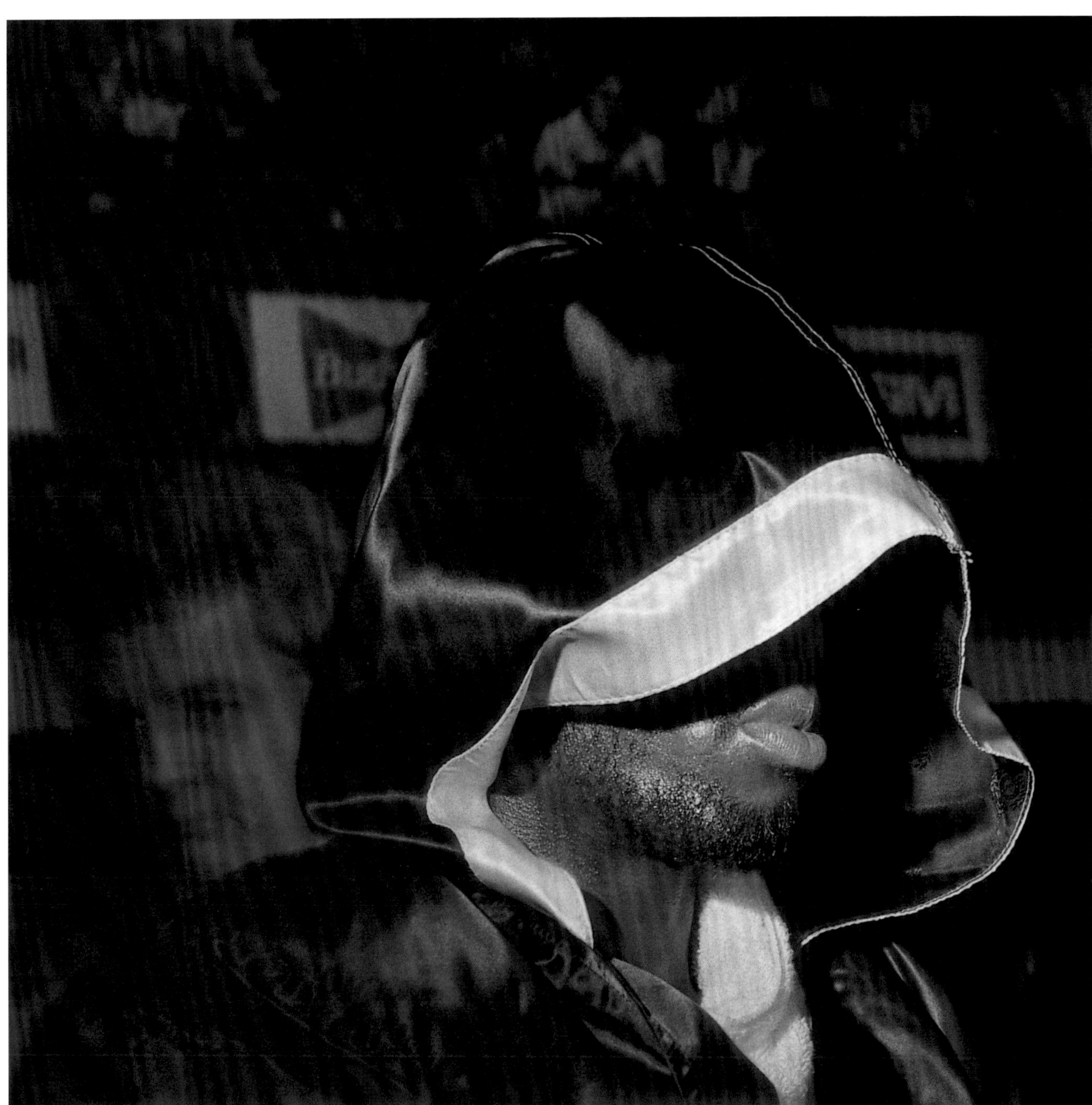

December 1994   Boxing, State Theater, Easton, Pennsylvania.

Standing behind one corner as the boxers wait for the bell, Fink shoots
without the flash to render the fighter's latent power with the delicate
backlight that traces the punishing bulk of the shoulders and arm. In
this moment of stasis with the boxer in deep shadow, we imagine the
pause is for preparing the mind as much as resting the body. Fink's view
from behind also delivers a negative judgement on the hapless opponent,
who registers as small, stooped and out of focus.

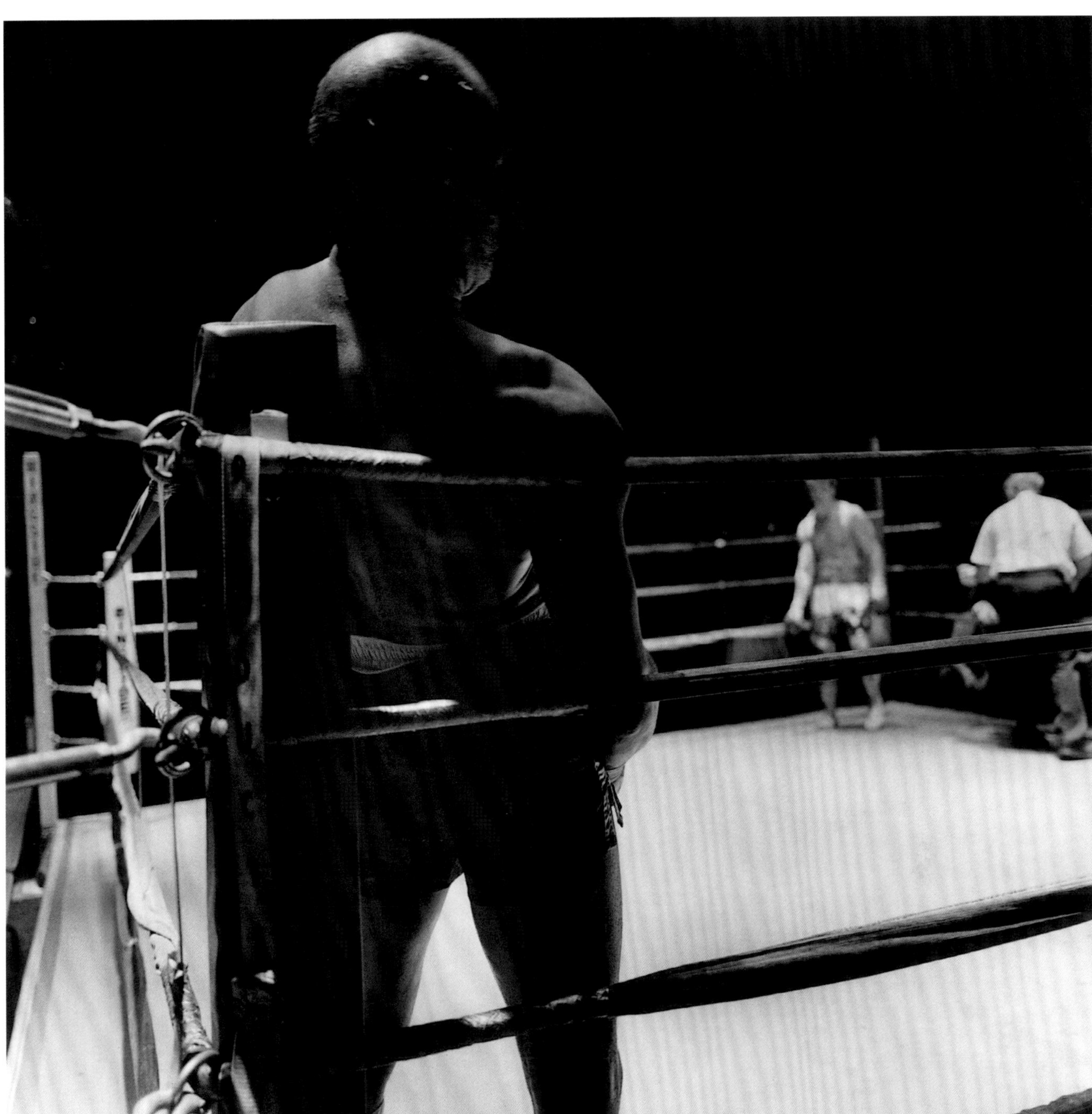

March 1995

Tampa, Florida.

Against his better judgement, Fink took a job from *Rolling Stone* to ride along with the Tampa police during the filming of *Cops,* a reality television programme. On the plane flight, he questioned his sanity, but when the police cruiser arrived on the scene of a knife fight, he found himself rushing ahead of the professionals, overly emboldened by the adrenaline. He was soon corrected. This man – 'in pain and pissed off' – had suffered a stab wound to the stomach.

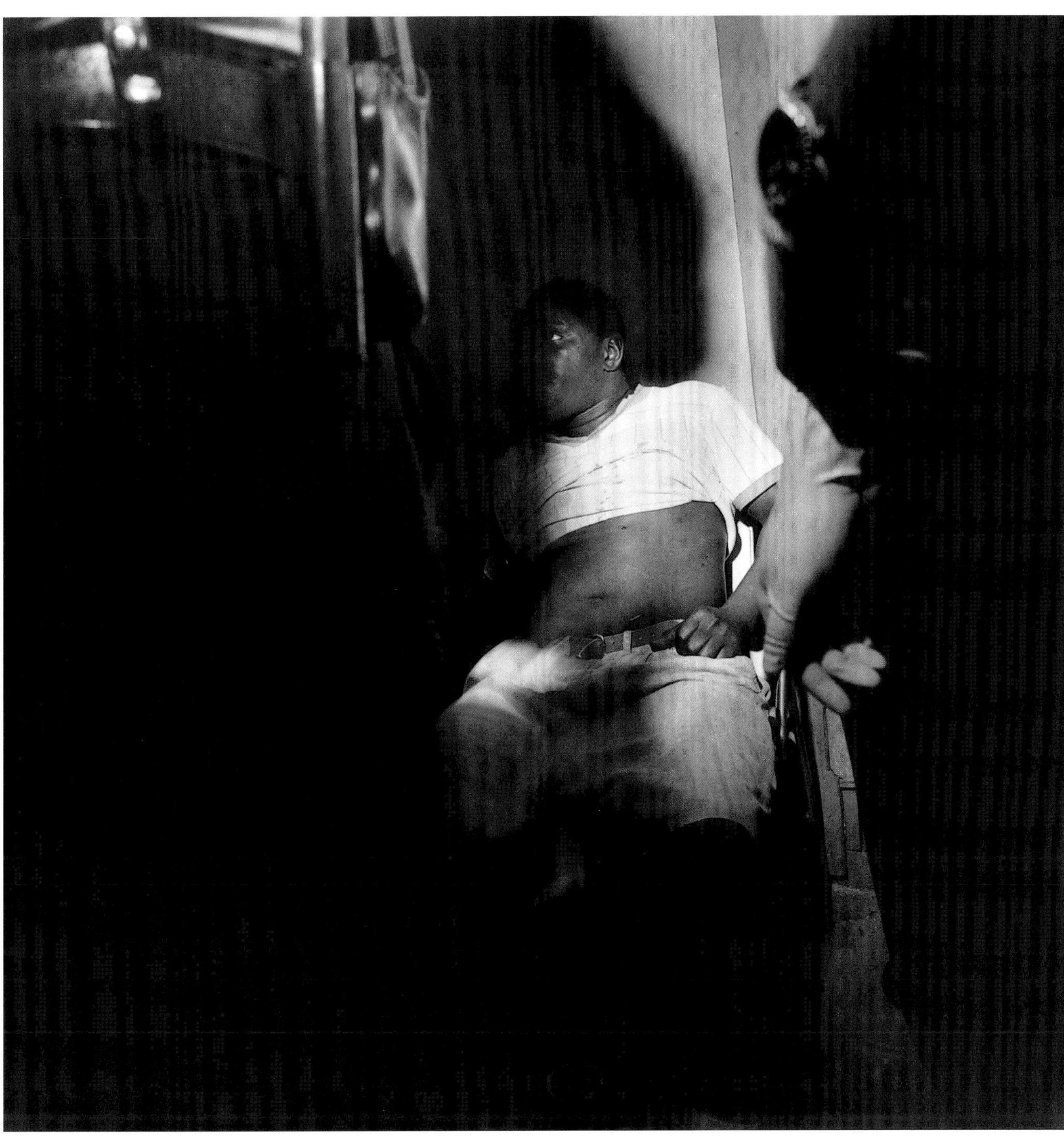

May 1995   Cleveland High School of the Arts, Ohio.

Commissioned by the George Gund Foundation to photograph a grant
recipient – an arts high school in inner-city Cleveland – Fink was surrounded
by the spectacle of highly motivated teenage performers. He describes this
image: 'Here are two kids who have a high degree of attention and intention,
and I have a flash which has a high degree of exquisite luck. I happened to
be the translator of the energy when it happened. Everything is there for the
absolute miracle of the decisive moment.'

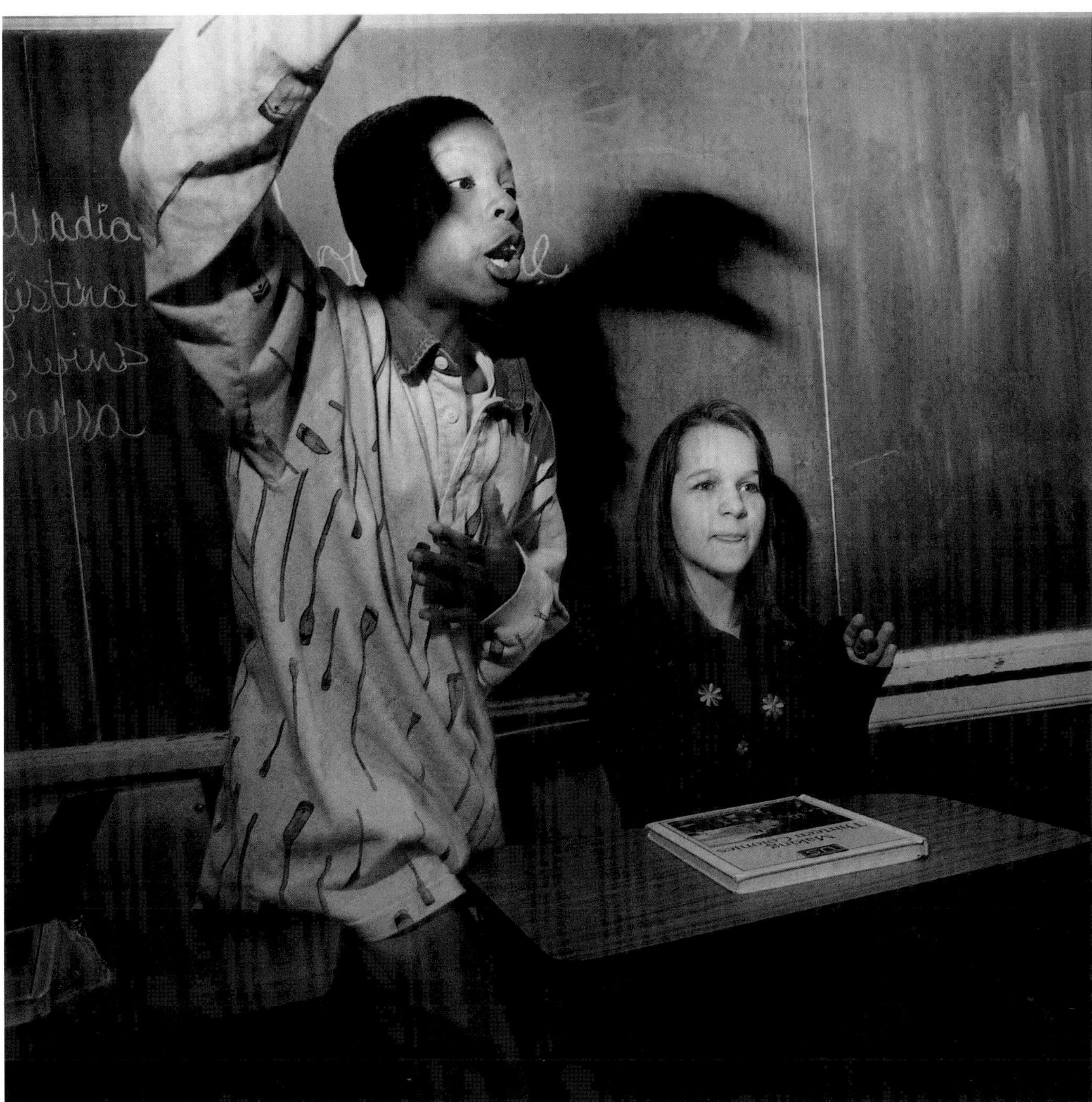

May 1995   Cleveland High School of the Arts, Ohio.

This picture, also made at the Cleveland High School of the Arts, describes the blissful, unselfconscious bonding of girls in a dance class. The sculptural clarity of the flash, combined with the background blur produced by a slow shutter speed, creates a dream-like space for these dancers, entranced and utterly absorbed in following the spontaneous suggestions of the music.

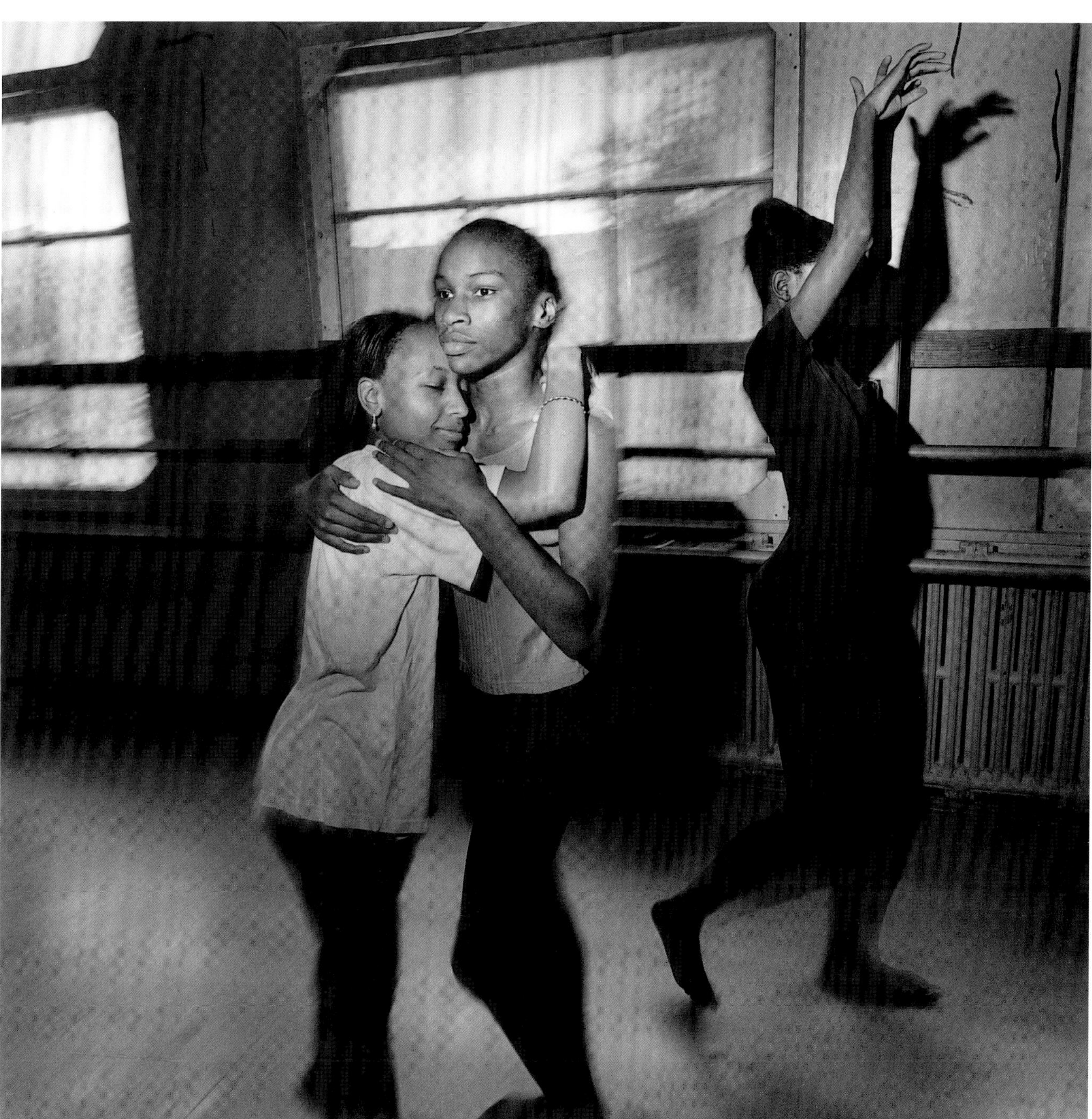

June 1995   Nate's Party, Martins Creek, Pennsylvania.

In an improbably idyllic episode straight out of Norman Rockwell's America, these boys took Fink with them on a summer jaunt to the local swimming hole. Cavorting on the banks of Martins Creek, the boys wrestle and, as Fink puts it, 'show their force' in typical teenage fashion. Stripping down for a dip, they enact a ritual surely performed by many generations before them.

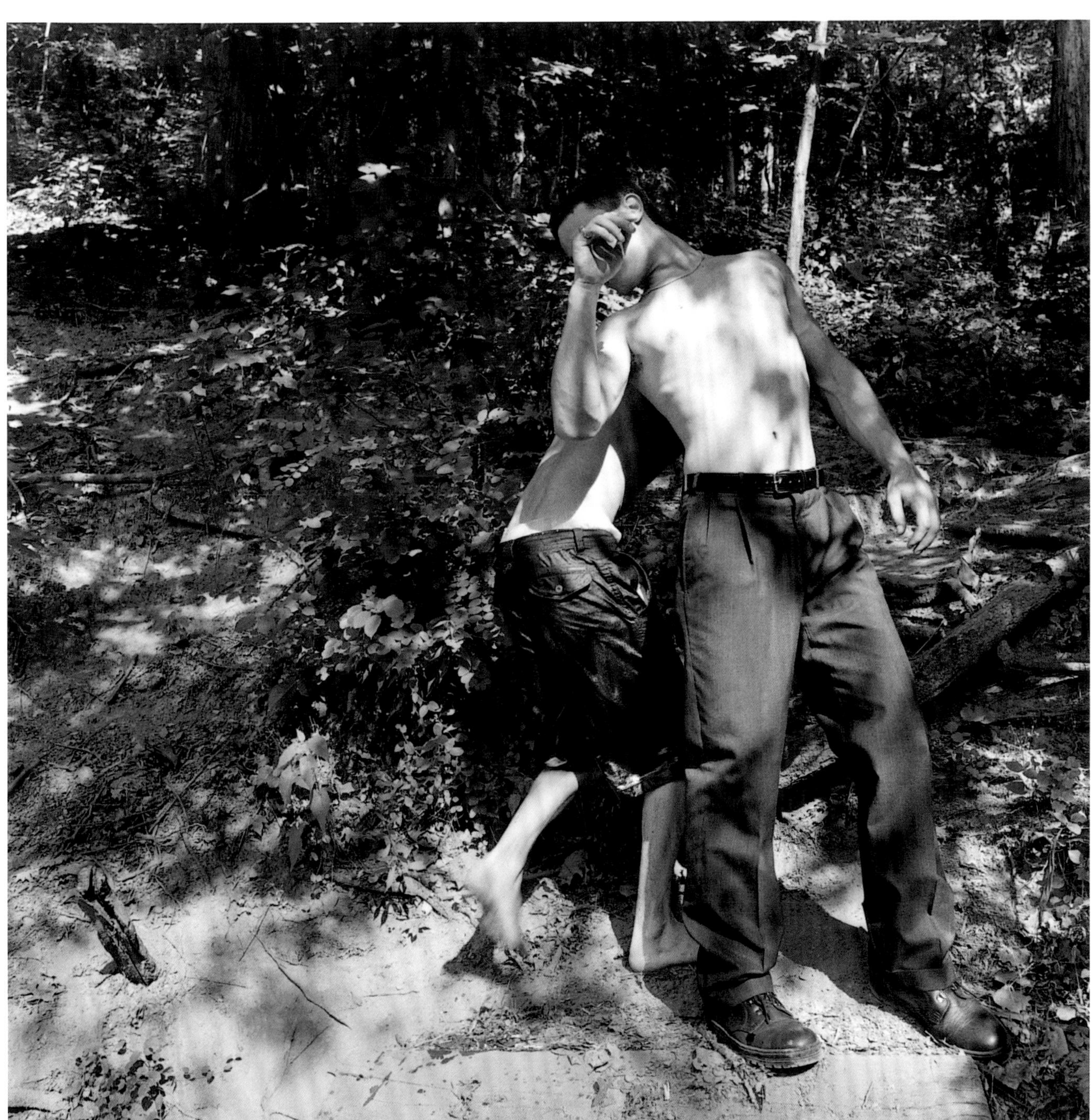

4 July 1995   Hummel's Dam, Pennsylvania.

With two broad-backed men huddled in conference around a keg at a Fourth of July party, this picture takes up the ancient allegorical figure of youth and age. The younger man listens respectfully, drawing his draught of beer, while his elder assumes an oratorical stance, giving special emphasis to his words of wisdom with a rhetorical gesture.

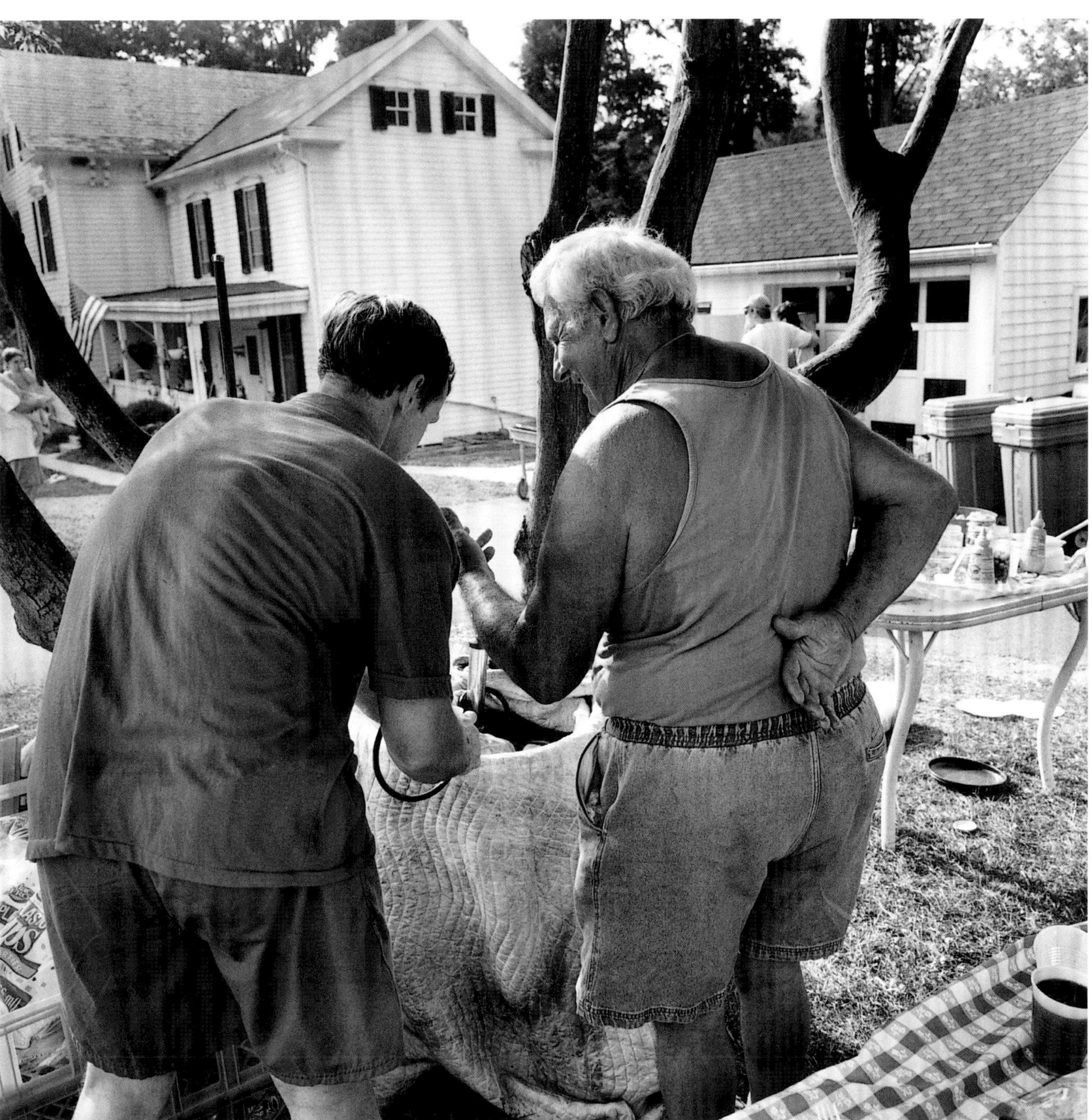

40

January 1996   Paris, France.

Fink's fashion photography has often featured the spectacle of the spectators, a strategy perhaps learned by example from the photographer Weegee. This image combines the strong geometry of the diagonally bisected frame with the undulating contours of the shawl. Just off-centre is the vortex of the picture, to which everything else is drawn: that impassive, flawlessly manicured hand, saturated with what Fink describes as 'a thickness of power'.

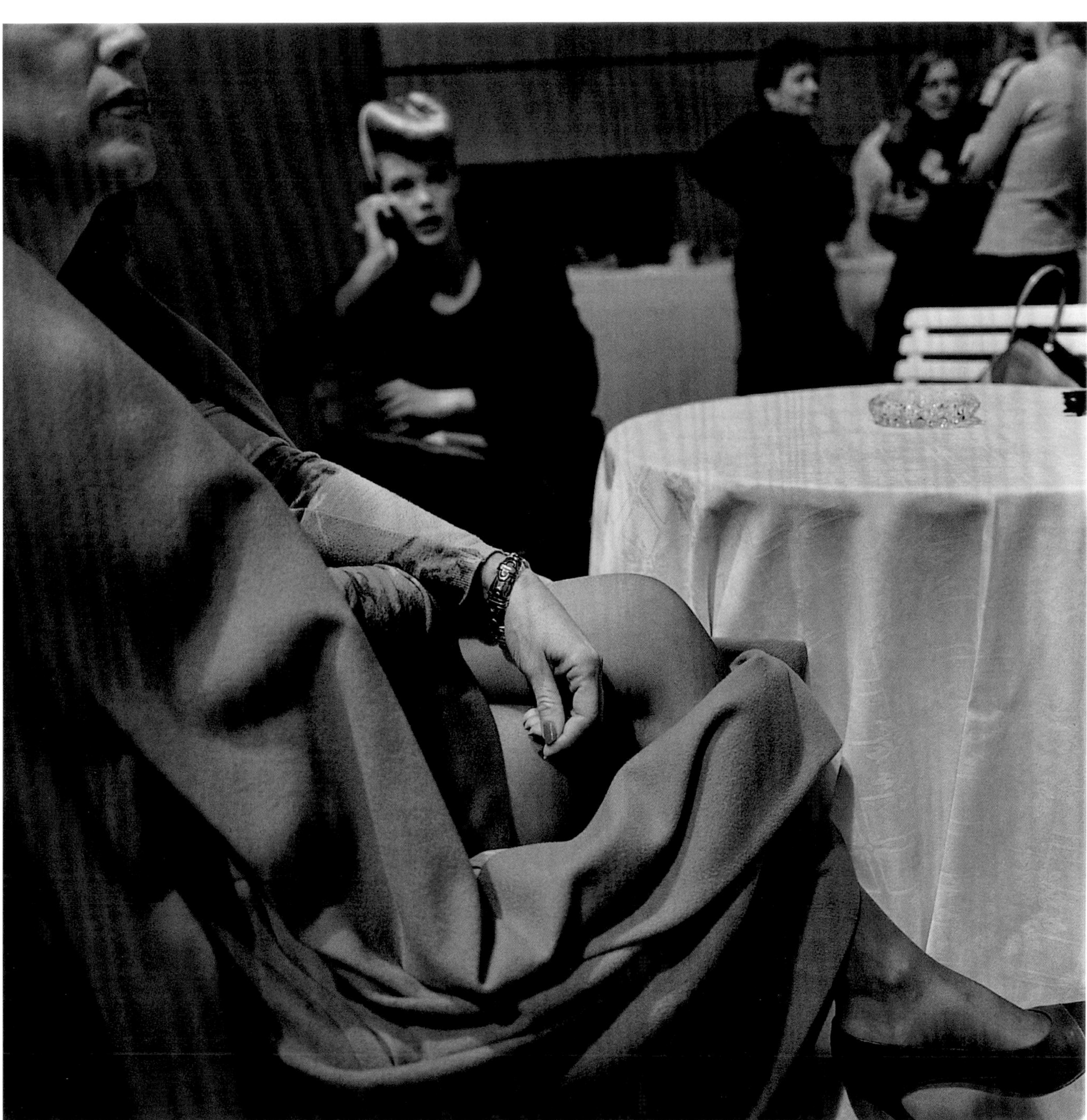

41

Christian Lacroix Haute Couture, Paris.

This picture exemplifies two of the things photography does best: it arrests the action of the moment so that formal or conceptual relationships can be visually savoured as they never could be in life, and it depicts the richness of surfaces. The descending diagonal sweep of the models' limbs matches the graceful detail of their gowns. The model's gesture, caught adjusting the frothy folds of her skirt, could hardly be lovelier, but it is the unifying tonal palette of black-and-white photography, optimally exposed and printed, that saturates this picture with elegance.

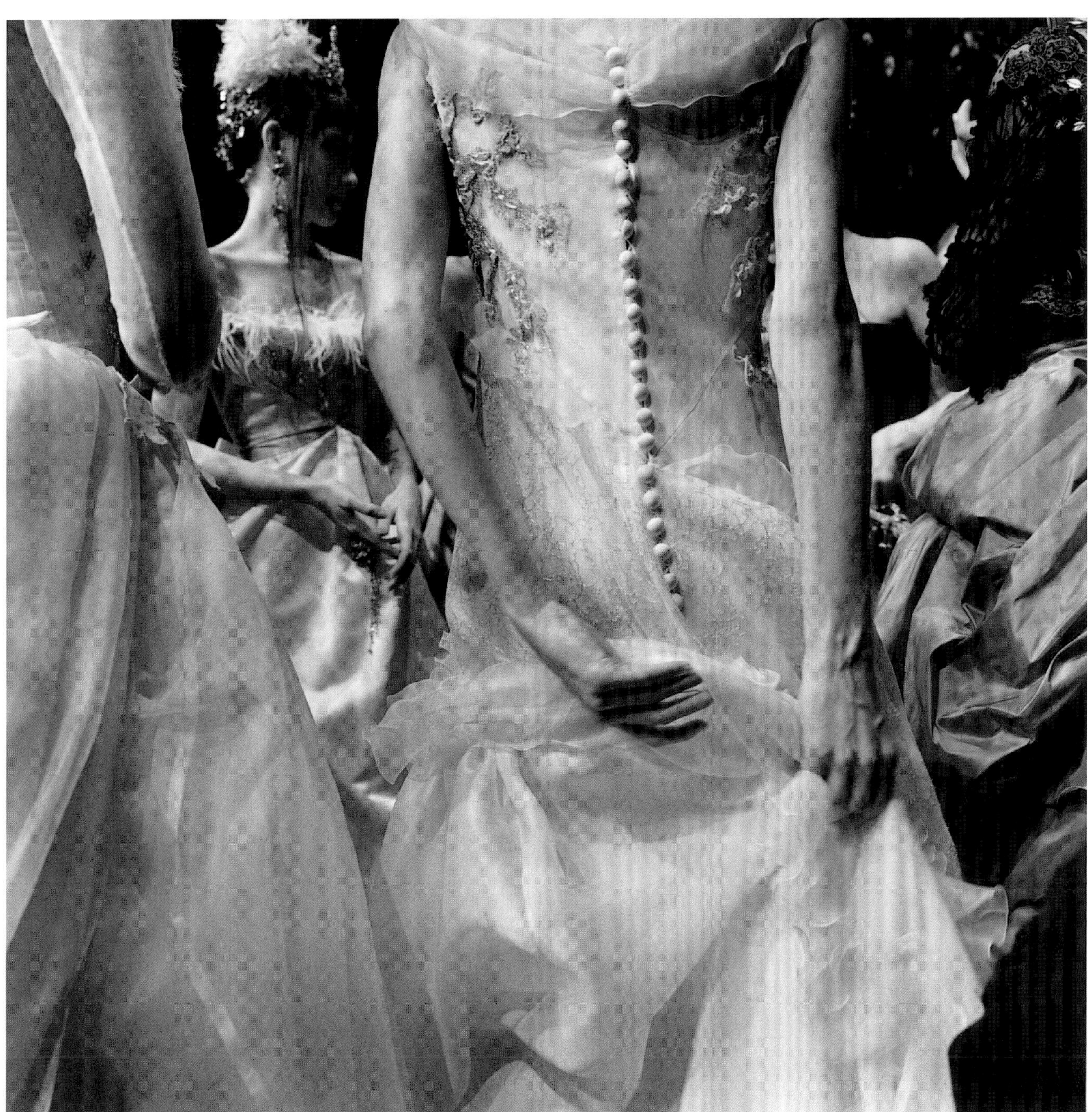

42

April 1996   American Planning Association Awards, New York City.

For this image, the flash was positioned behind the action. Since Fink's pictures involve the convergence of three factors – the position of the instantaneous flash, the place of the photographer and the objects moving through their respective fields – there is no knowing exactly what will fall into shadow or be highlighted within the photographic frame. These qualities of accident, chance and spontaneous discovery are central to Fink's concept of his art. He was certainly aware that the stoic waiter's pose would double that of the statue to the left, and he surely noticed the face of the painted figure vainly emoting in their direction, but the gigantic silhouette of the party-goers, blithely unaware of the strange drama occurring around them, was the wild card. Chance once again favours the prepared mind.

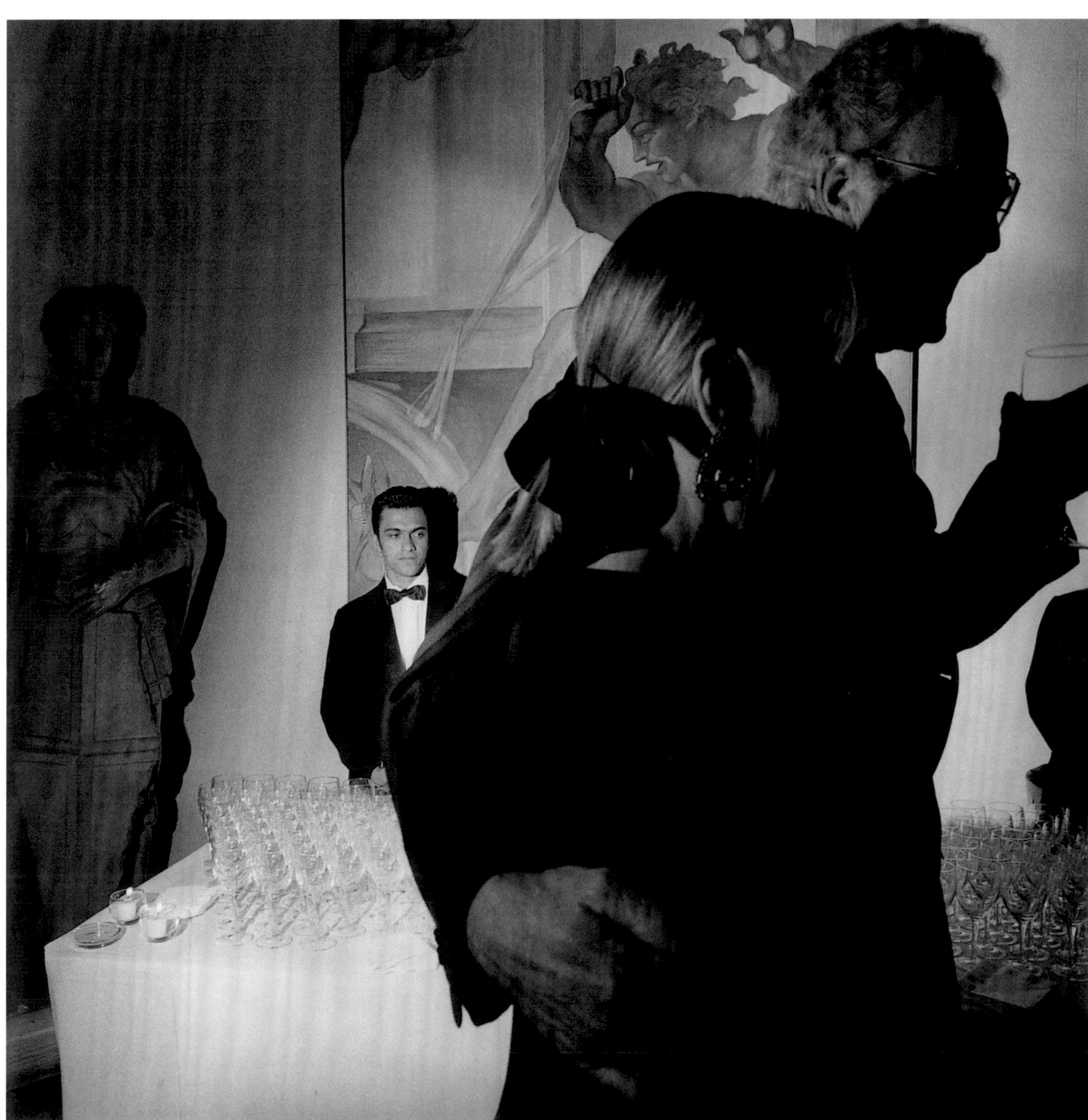

43 | April 1996 | Edwardian Ball, Frick Museum, New York City.

The complications of space in this image are the product of Fink's intuitive and experimental approach to lighting. In this instance, he used three or four radio-controlled strobes placed around the room. Space seems illogically compressed by the occurrence of bright areas in both foreground and background, which the eye wants to read as occupying the same spatial plane. With virtually no middle tones to model their forms, these women become graphically fused together in a cubist jigsaw.

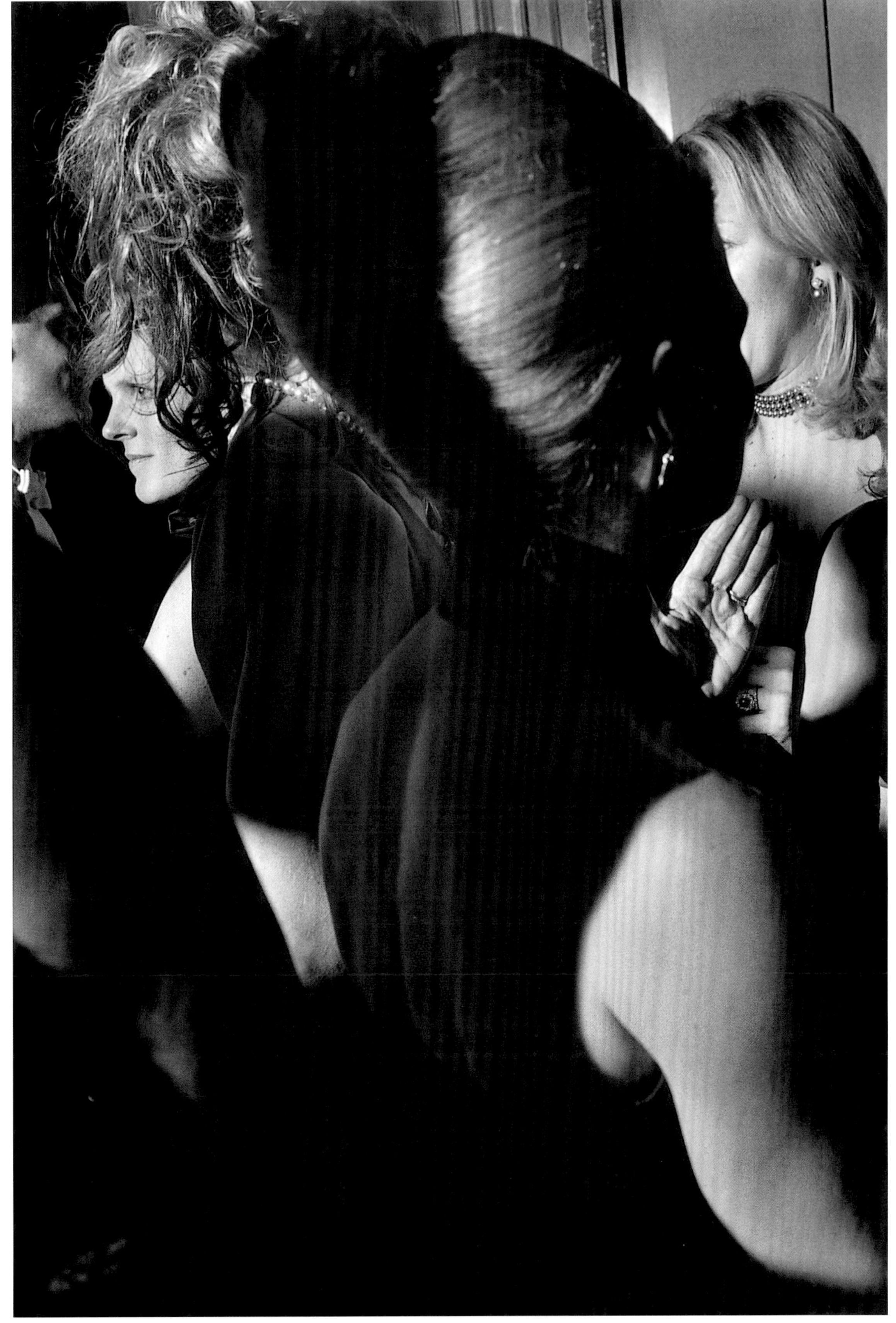

June 1996　　Elaine's, New York City.

Although Fink has worked frequently for fashion houses over the years, he is more than willing to criticize the vanity and decadence he associates with the industry – in fact, his employers have usually sought him out expressly for his edgy, antagonistic view of glamour. He has shot fashion both straight (without intervention or manipulation) and as staged tableaux (as in this photograph). Here he chooses Brassaï's favoured strategy of doubling the scene in a mirror, which in this case artificially replicates a group of people who are already monotonously interchangeable in their beauty and glamour.

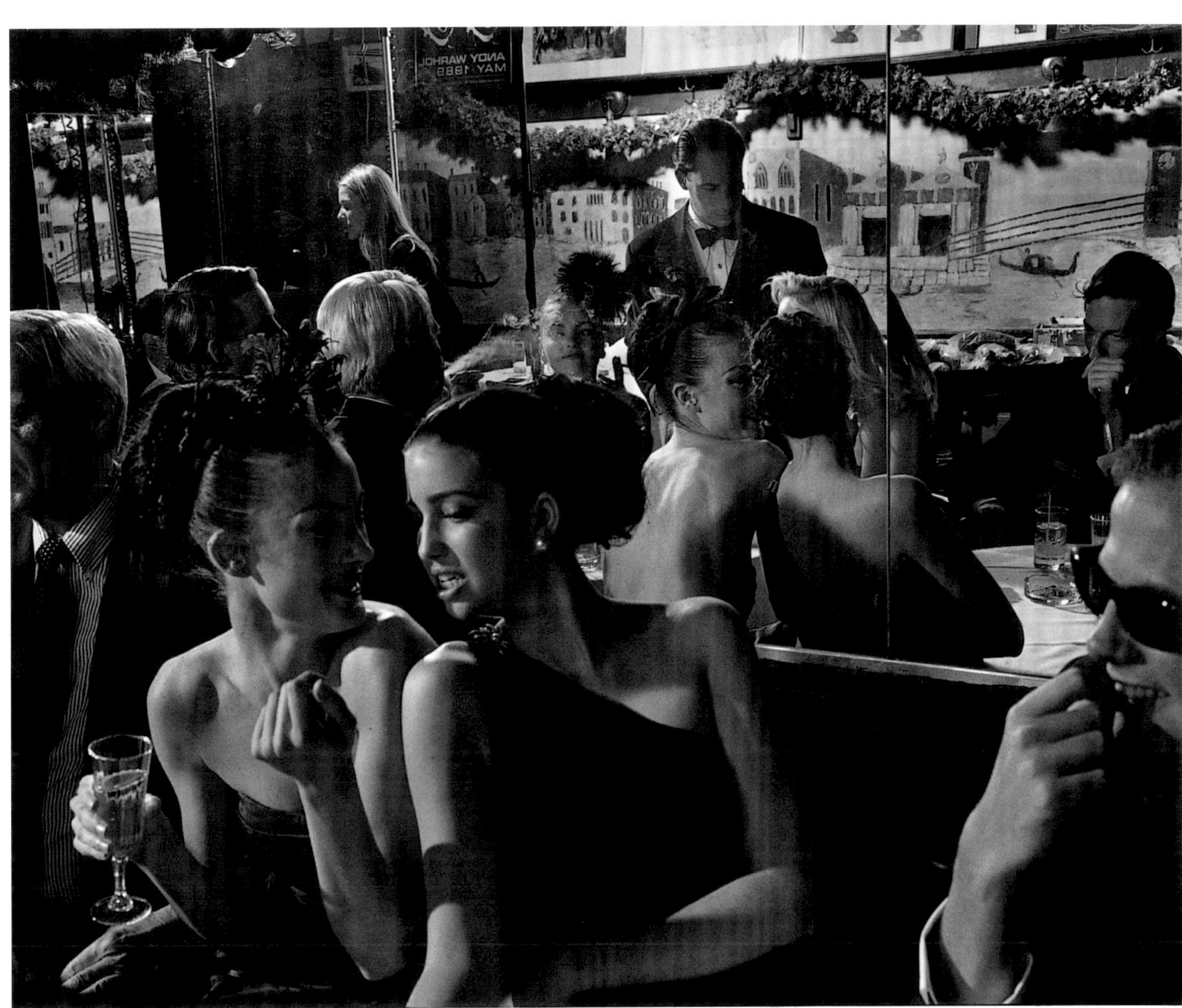

45 September 1996 Sante d'Orazio and Kara Young's Wedding, New York City.

While Fink cannot be said to be a photographer who emphasizes geometric relationships within the picture above other concerns, he often composes the content of his frame to exploit the natural geometric power of the square. This picture is organized on a strong diagonal that reaches from corner to corner. The sensuous, undulating play of limbs is punctuated at dead centre by the circular form of the man's hand: the navel of the image.

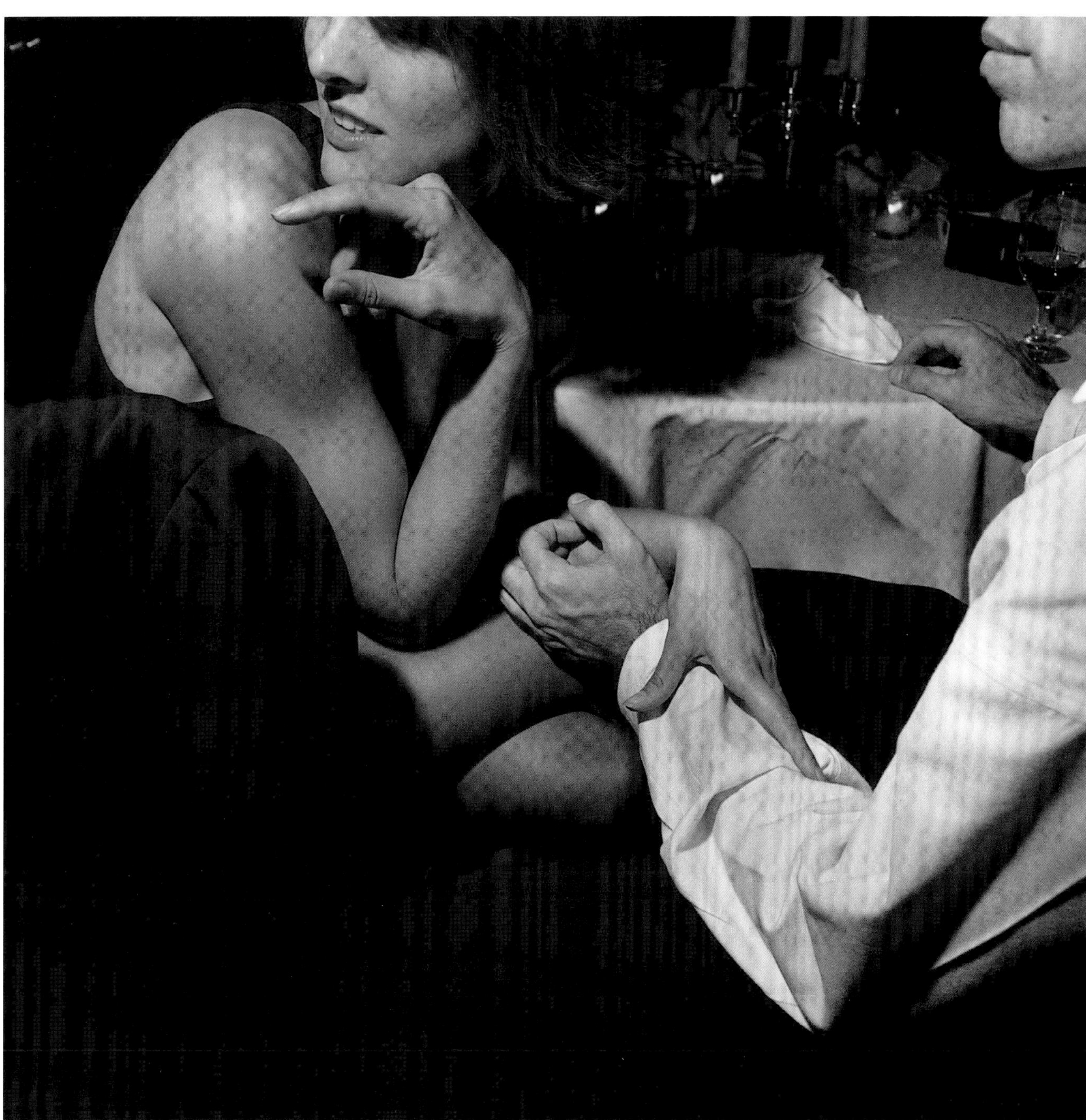

   September 1996   Sante d'Orazio and Kara Young's Wedding, New York City.

This girl's face, illuminated and transfixed in the midst of her mundane surroundings by the sight of something unseen, resembles a scene from the Childhood of the Virgin. Fink achieves this orchestration of light and dark by manipulating both the negative (using the flash to illuminate discrete areas) and the positive print (by shaping the print through localized exposure – burning and dodging). These technical actions are so seamlessly enacted that viewers see only what the photographer intends: the miraculous quality of the 'natural' moment, unified by the black-and-white medium.

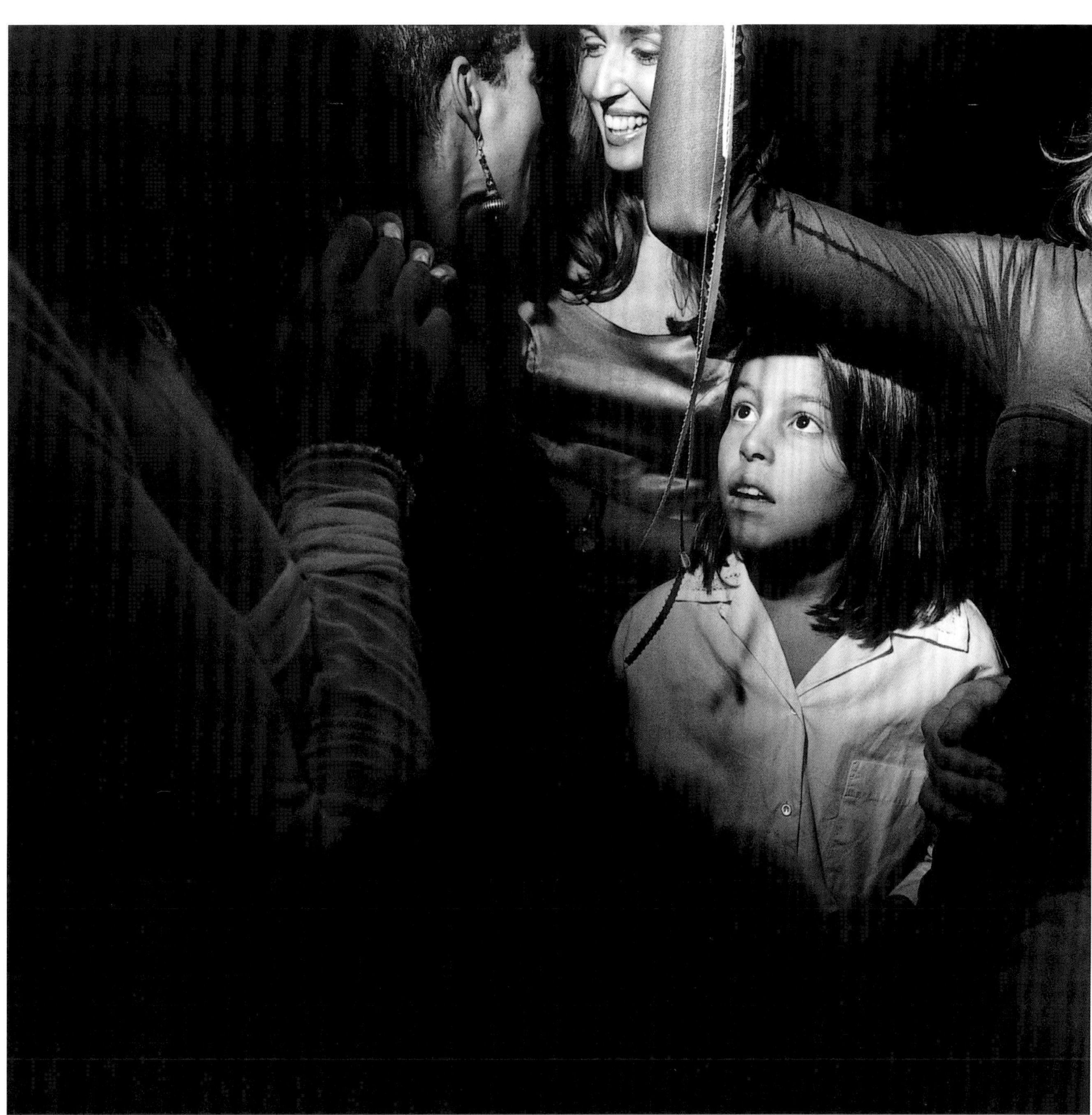

June 1997 | Ferretti Wedding, Allentown, Pennsylvania.

Fink's wedding pictures are not restricted to the tropes of the genre. In fact, he steadfastly avoids the territory of standard wedding pictures, such as the groom looking at his watch or the bride having her hair done. This surreal image portrays the swollen legs of a grandmother, as they seem to float magically in a void. The floor falls away in the absence of light, making her appear to be spontaneously rising out of the frame.

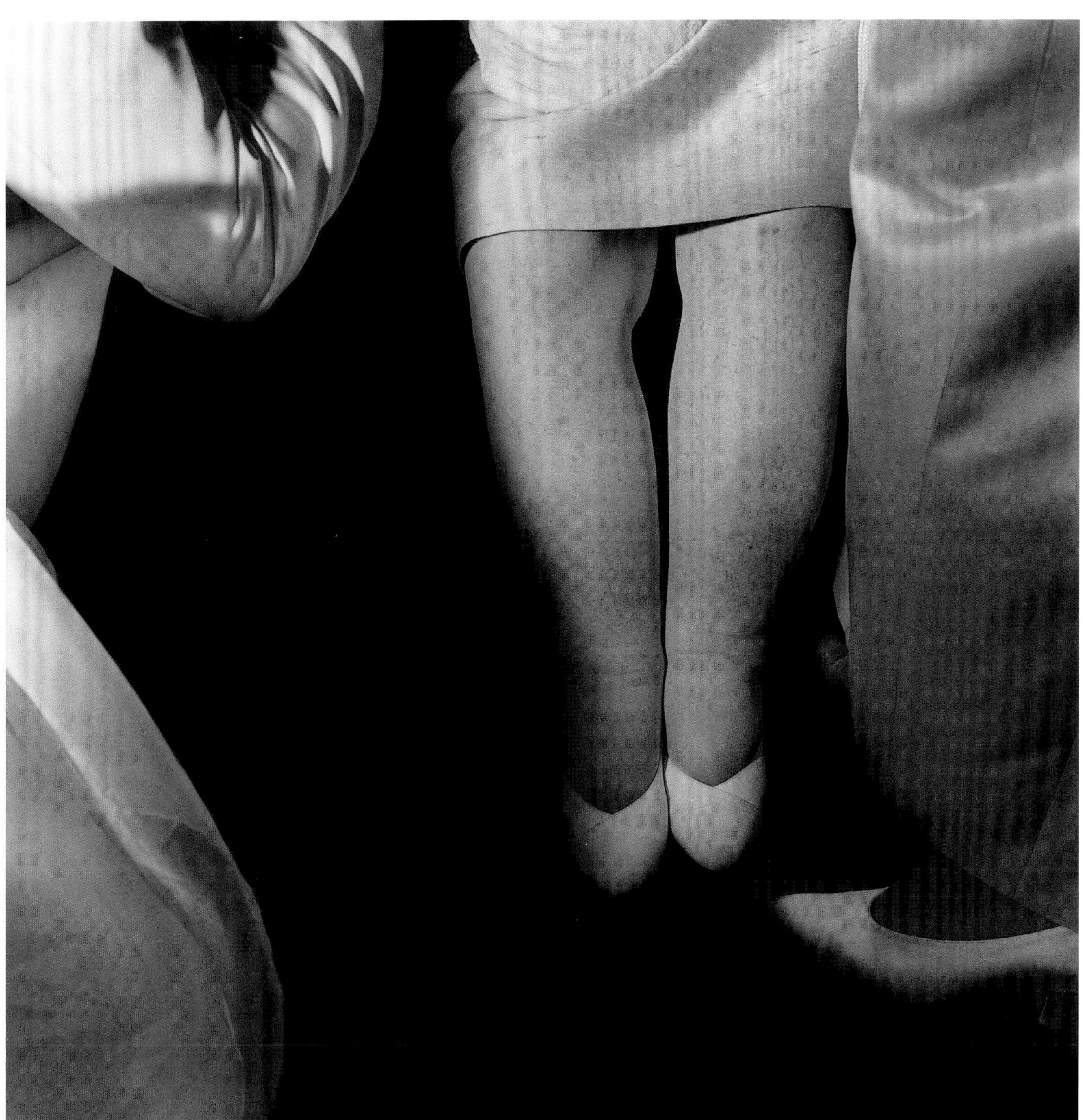

June 1997 | Ferretti Wedding, Allentown, Pennsylvania.

In this photograph, the flash plays tricks with scale by obliterating the middle ground. The strobe-lit faces (at varying distances from the camera) all appear to come forward in the visual field, while everything in shadow recedes. Disembodied by deep shadow, these wedding guests are transformed into an amusing rogues' gallery: a collage of caricatures of gaiety.

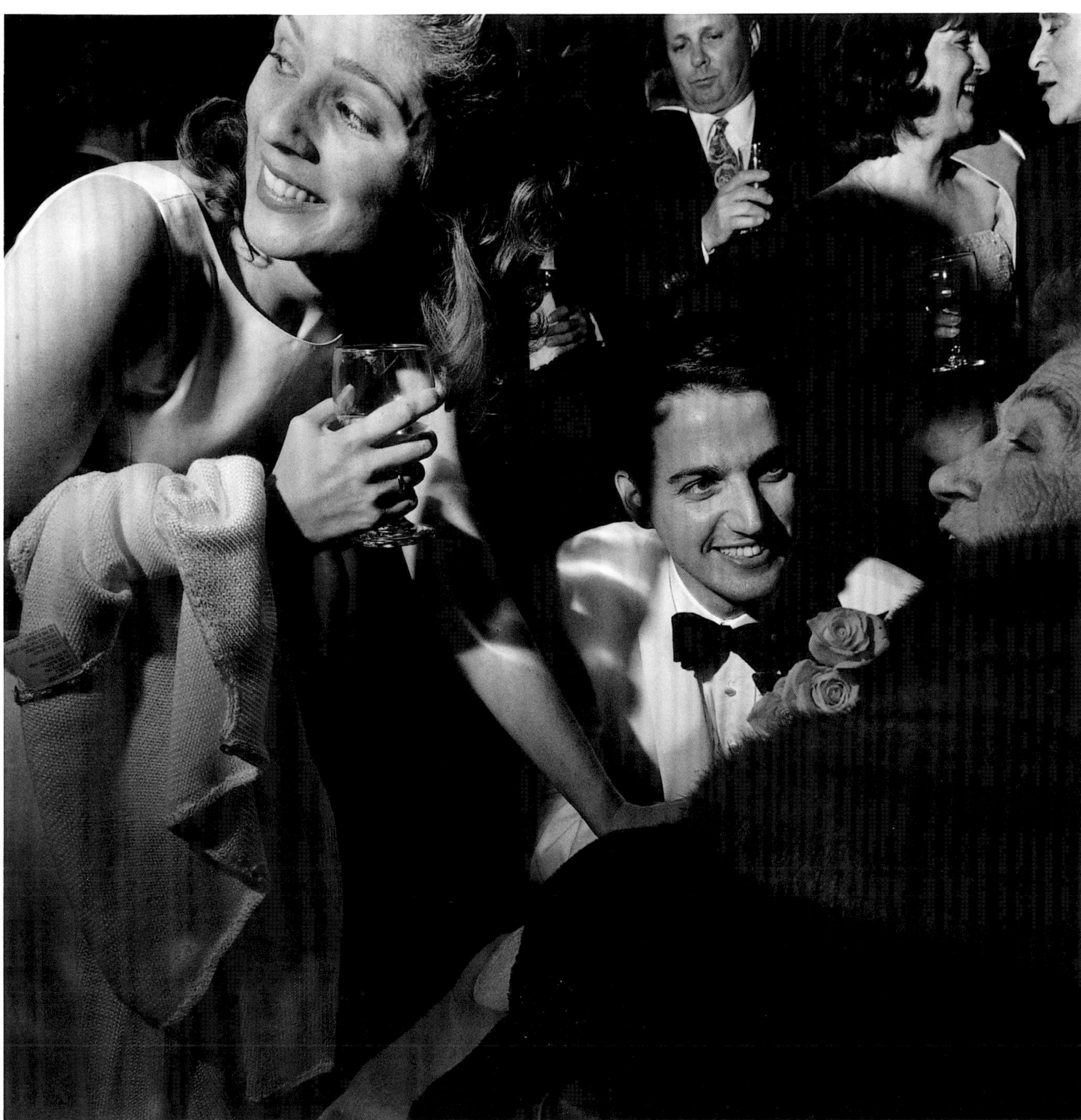

March 1998 | Paris, France.

Here, Fink stepped back from his usual place in the midst of the crowd and photographed Parisian nightlife (in this case, a party thrown by one of the fashion houses) in the spirit of Brassaï's mysterious *Paris de Nuit* (1932). On this occasion he worked with the light provided by a constellation of low-wattage hanging bulbs to create a naturalistic, atmospheric view into the smoky interior of the cavernous room.

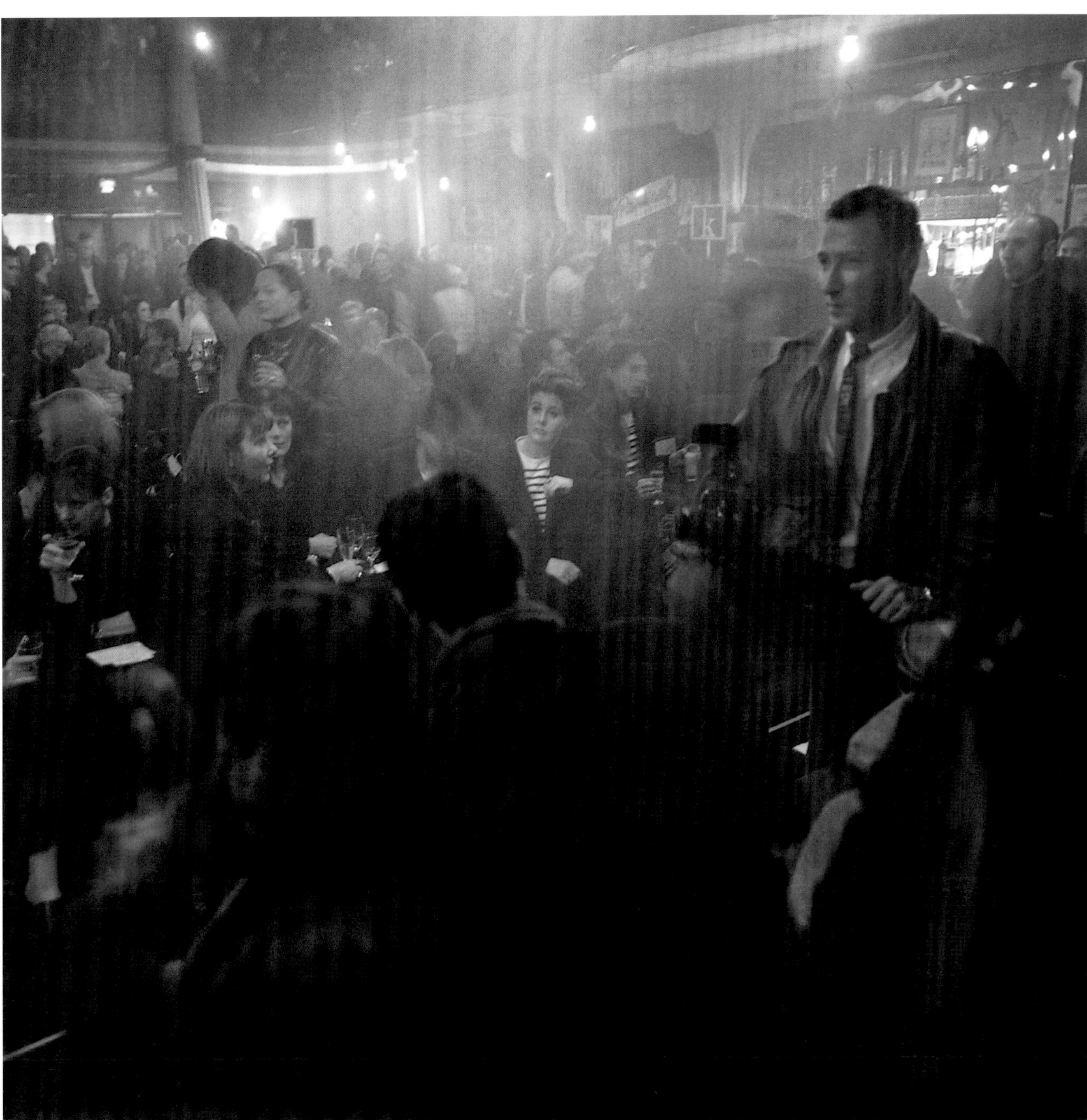

March 1998 | Outside Chanel House, Paris, France.

Fink has made a career out of using his artistic licence to act on his old subversive ideals, here by cutting off the heads of the fashionistas and exposing the inelegance of the mink-coated fashion maven with the unshapely legs. The spindly phallus at the centre stands in as a rude gesture.

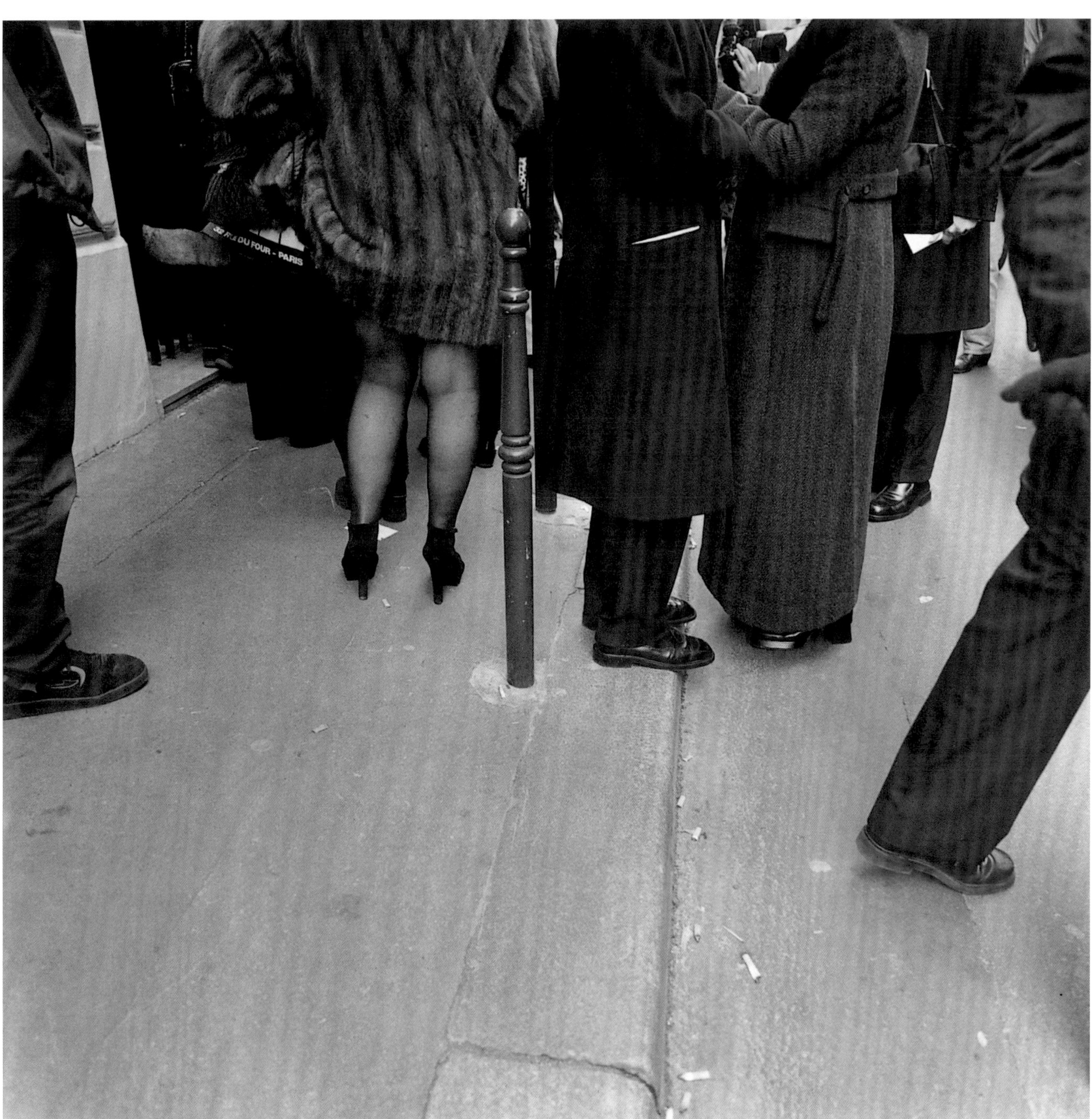
RUE DU FOUR - PARIS

July 1998

Thierry Mugler Men's Ready-to-Wear, Paris.

Here the looming, shadowy figure in the exquisite suit is Mr Mugler himself, scrutinizing one of his models in a state of undress. The figures face each other with the static tension of a Wild West showdown but, instead of a challenge between gunfighters, the competition sets Apollonian beauty against the power of wealth and rank.

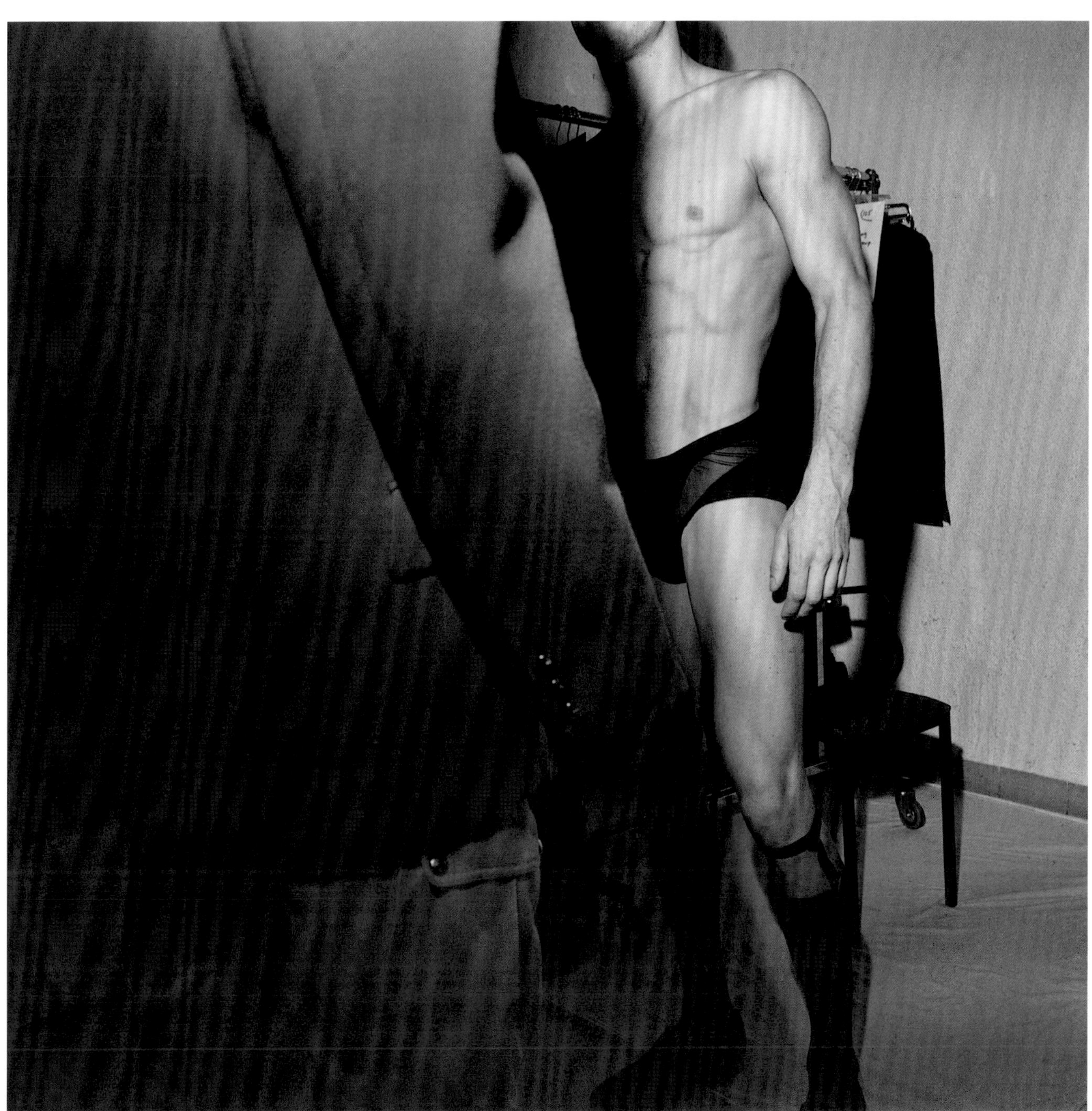

September 1998   Joyce and Antoine's Wedding, New York.

Photographed from below, with the soaring trees behind her, this formidable woman becomes a goddess of nature, a Diana figure: powerful, beautiful and unobtainable. The video camera has replaced the goddess's bow and arrow, but she is on the hunt nonetheless.

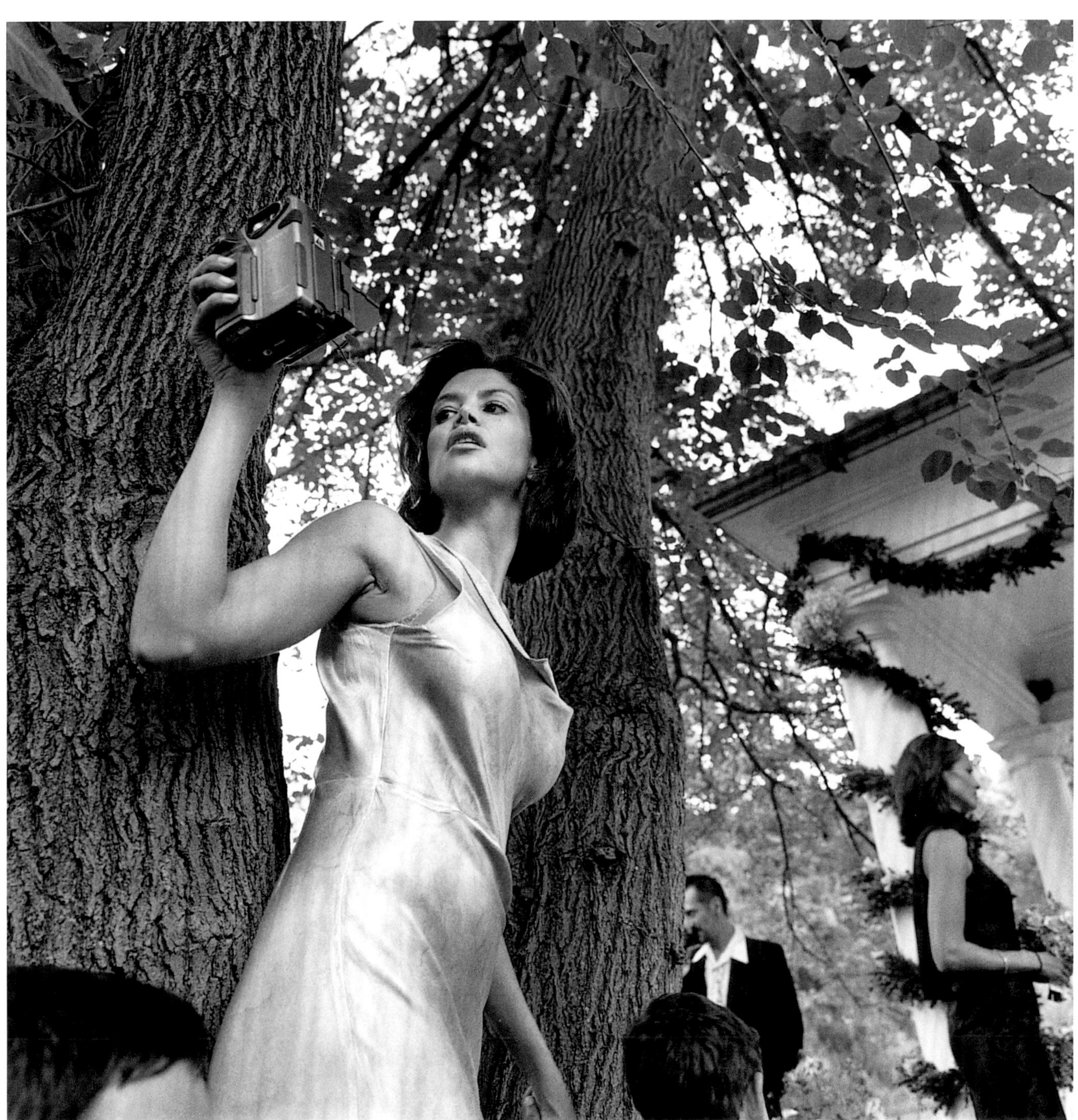

October 1998

Grubman Wedding, Hotel Pierre, New York City.

Pictures of children are rarely enigmatic, but this one provokes great curiosity about the psychology of this innocent flower girl. Revealed in the raking light of the strobe, there is something menacing in her private isolation within the crowd of wedding revellers, all straining for a glimpse of the bride and groom. The seated man seems impossibly oblivious to the intensity of her gaze.

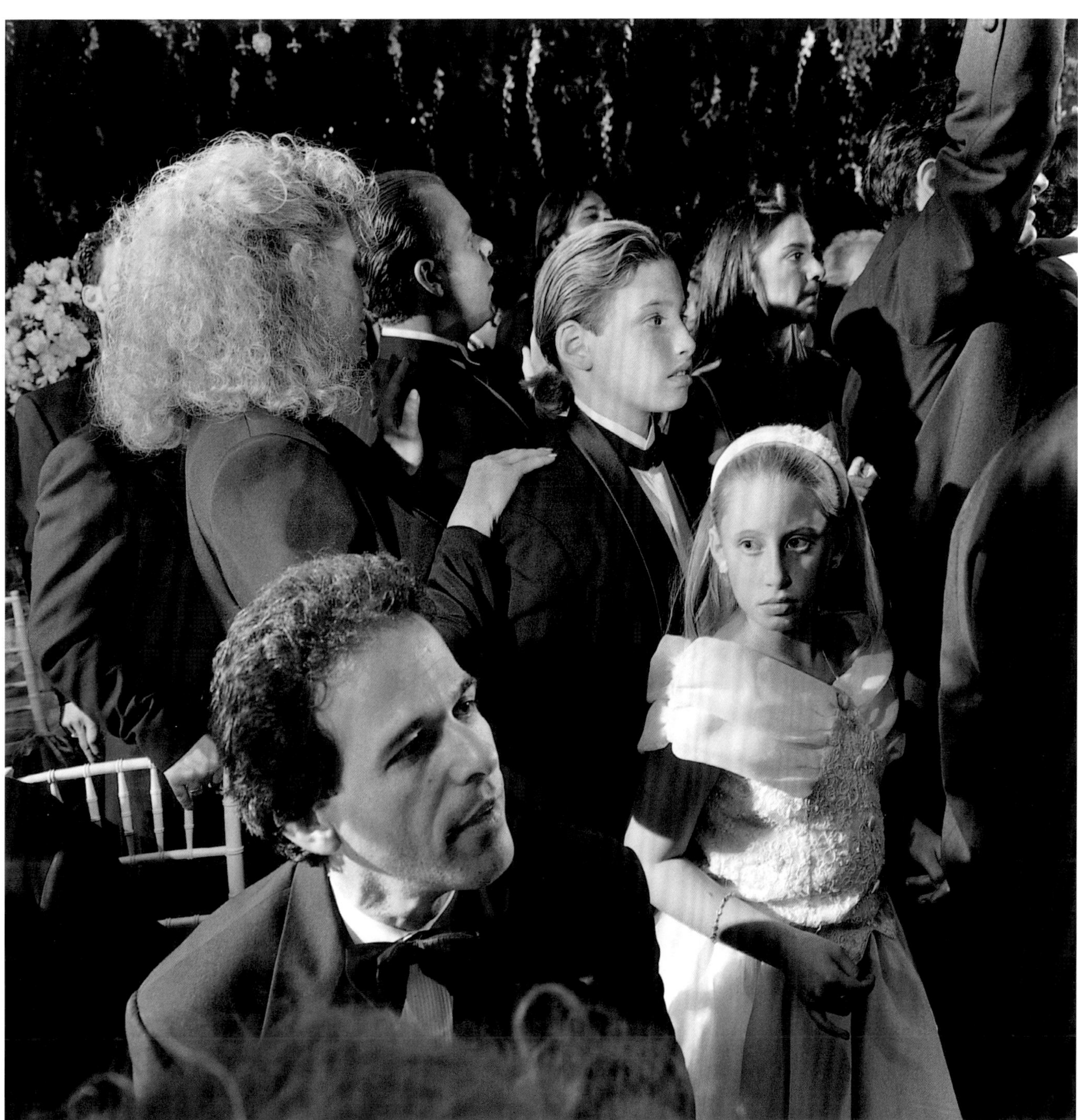

 October 1998   Grubman Wedding, Hotel Pierre, New York City.

Fink remains an old-school Marxist even on commissioned jobs. In wilfully 'defacing' the portrait of this couple by obliterating their camera smiles with the ostentatious centrepiece, Fink is up to some of his old agitational tricks. In *The English at Home* (1936), the photographer Bill Brandt presented an eviscerating portrait of the British aristocracy through the portrayal of their armies of servants. Fink's rich Americans, on the other hand, are defined by what they own and consume. The display of wealth has never looked so vulgar.

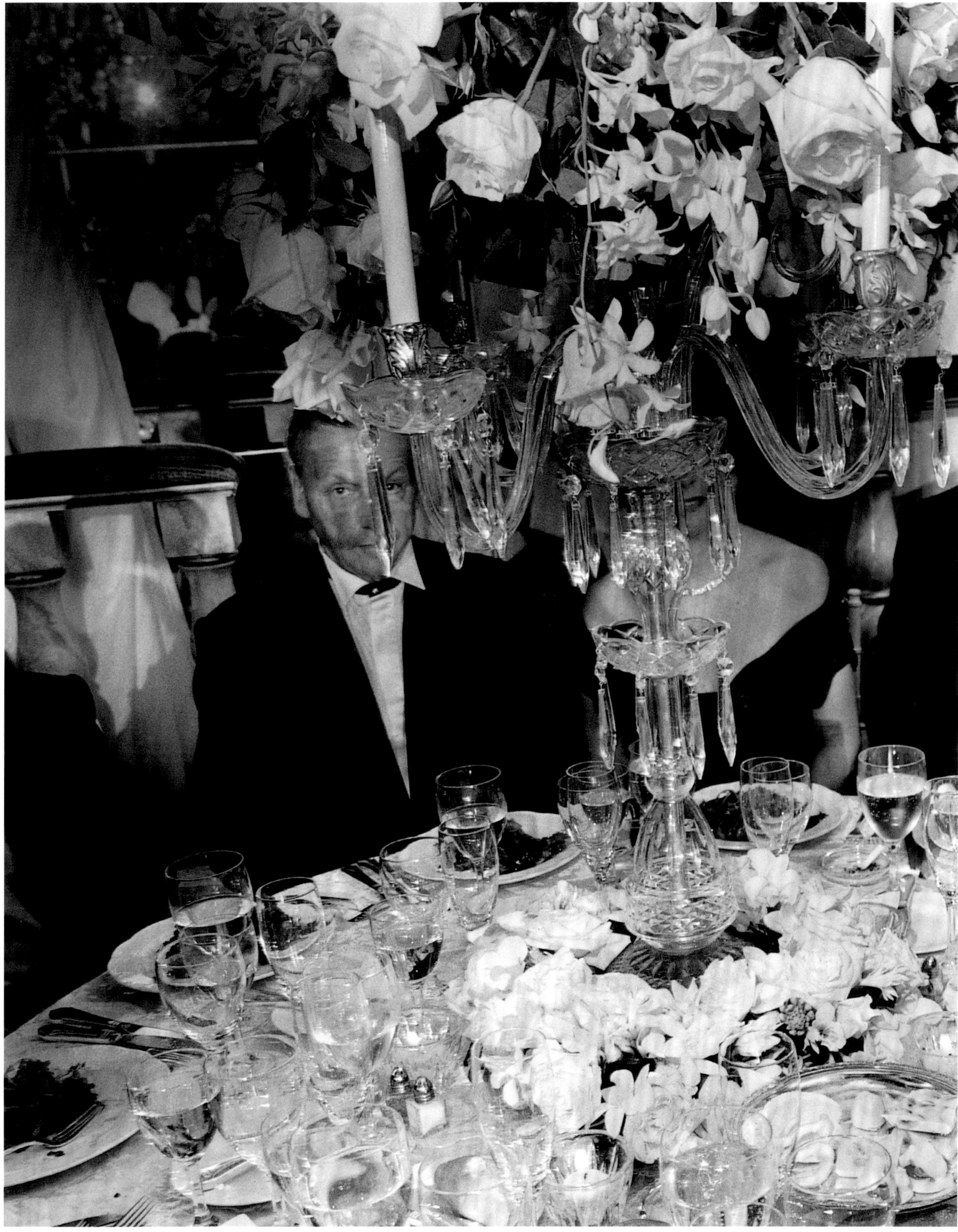

December 1998   Melzer Wedding, New York.

In this photograph, Fink's flash arrests the preoccupation of an elderly couple waiting in the receiving line. The woman wears the poignant, bewildered, beatified expression of a saint in a Renaissance altarpiece, while the man looks (perhaps suspiciously) at the black gentleman entering from the right.

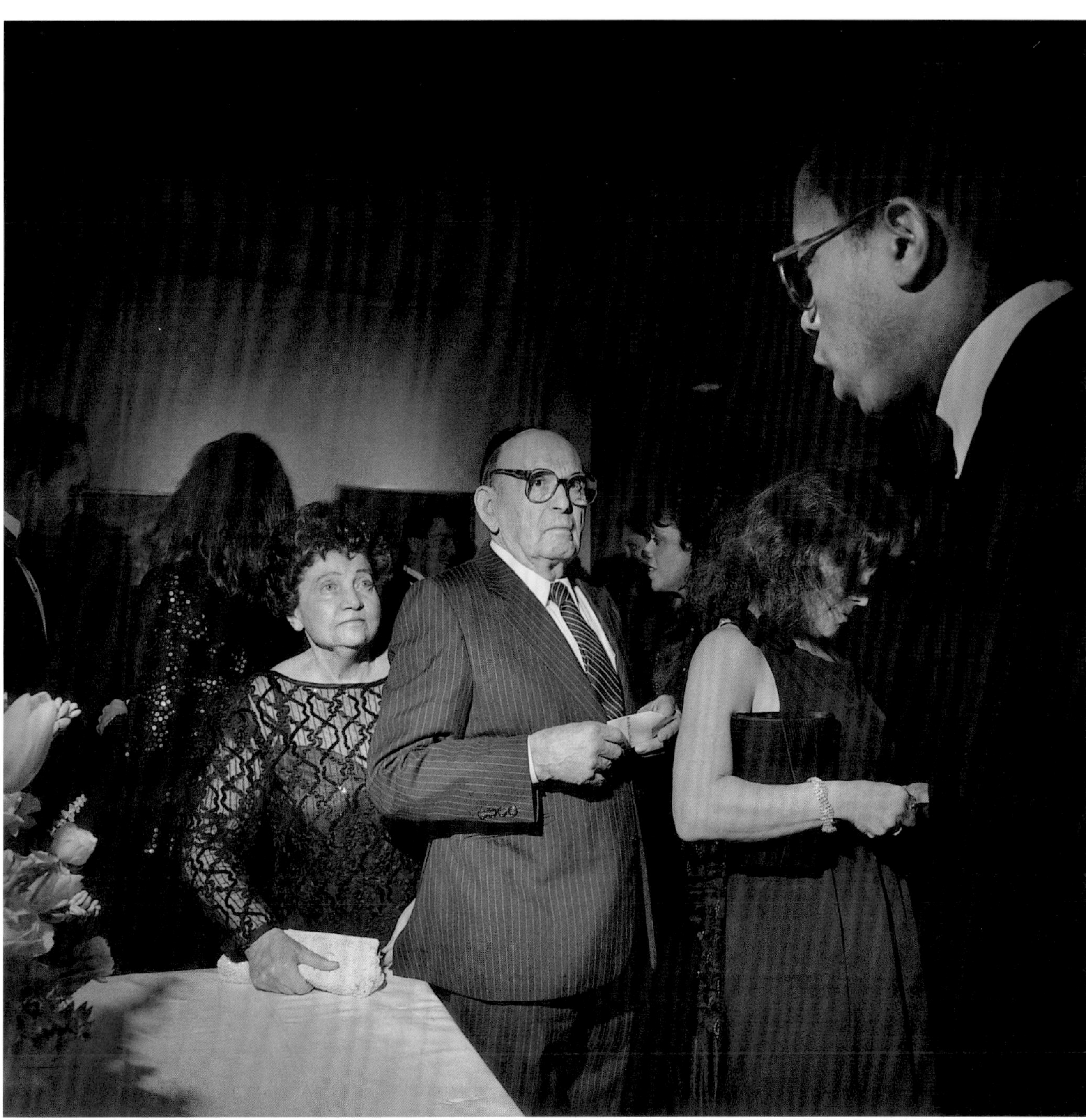

1941   Born 11 March to a middle-class Jewish family in Brooklyn, New York.
            Father is an insurance agent, mother is an organizer for social and political
            causes.

1954   Takes up photography as a hobby and builds an enlarger with a neigh-
            bourhood friend.

1959   Enrols at Coe College, Iowa. Lasts several months before dropping out to
            hitchhike around the country.

1960–63   Returns to New York City and photographs for Lexington School for the
            Deaf. Publishes his first pictures in *Jubilee,* a progressive Catholic maga-
            zine. Becomes a staff photographer for Three Lions Agency, a picture
            agency for the Catholic press.

1961–63   Studies privately with Lisette Model.

1963–68   Curates photography shows at Columbia University and other local venues
            for the peace movement.

1964   Teaches photography at Haryou Act Anti-Poverty Program in Harlem.

1965–72   Begins teaching photography at Parsons School of Design and the New
            School, New York.

1969   Marries painter Joan Snyder. Begins photographing high-society
            Manhattan black-tie parties. Starts regularly using flash method. Officially
            enters art world with solo show at Paley and Low, an emerging SoHo
            gallery, New York.

1970   Included in group show, curated by John Szarkowski, at the Museum of
            Modern Art, New York.

1973   Moves to farm in Martins Creek, eastern Pennsylvania.

1976   Receives first Guggenheim fellowship. Begins photographing locally in
            Martins Creek.

1977   Visiting Professor at Yale School of Fine Arts, New Haven, Connecticut.

1978   Receives fellowship from National Endowment for the Arts.

1978–83   Teaches photography at the Cooper Union School of Art, New York.

1979   First solo exhibition at the Museum of Modern Art, New York.
            Receives a second Guggenheim fellowship. Birth of daughter, Molly.

1981   Second solo exhibition at Museum of Modern Art, New York.

1984   Publishes first book, *Social Graces*, essay by Larry Fink.

1986   Receives second fellowship from National Endowment for the Arts.

1986–date Teaches at Bard College, Annandale, New York.

1987   Begins photographing local boxing culture in the Philadelphia area.

1990   Marries shiatsu master Pia Staniek.

1993   Solo exhibition, *Les Rencontres de Photographie*, Arles, France. Retrospective
            exhibition at Musée de l'Elysée, Lausanne, Switzerland.

1994   Retrospective exhibition, *Fotografie Forum*, Frankfurt, Germany. Returns
            for a further year as Visiting Professor at Yale School of Fine Arts, New
            Haven, Connecticut. Solo exhibition at Whitney Museum of Art, New
            York.

1997   Retrospective exhibition at the Musée de la Photographie, Charleroi,
            southwest Belgium. Publishes the book *Boxing*, essay by Bert Sugar.

2000   Publishes *Runway,* a collection of fashion photographs. Marries artist
            Martha Posner.

2002   Publishes second edition of *Social Graces*. Awarded Honorary Degree of
            Doctor of Fine Arts, College for Creative Studies, College of Art and Design,
            Detroit, Michigan. Solo exhibition at Jersey City Museum, New Jersey.

2004   Publishes *Forbidden Pictures 7/19/01* and *Woolrich Roadtrip, New York, NY to
            Woolrich, PA*. Solo exhibitions at Edwynn Houk Gallery, New York City and
            powerHouse Gallery, New York City.

Front jacket
Joyce and Antoine's Wedding, New York.
September 1998 (see no. 52)

Phaidon Press Limited
Regent's Wharf
All Saints Street
London N1 9PA

Phaidon Press Inc.
180 Varick Street
New York NY 10014

www.phaidon.com

First published 2005
©2005 Phaidon Press Limited

ISBN 0 7148 4022 X

Designed by Pentagram
Printed in China